Mighty Mom's Secrets for Raising Super Kids

by
Gwendolyn Mitchell Diaz

RIVER OAK
PUBLISHING

Tulsa, Oklahoma

Mighty Mom's Secrets for Raising Super Kids:
Guidelines for the Adventure Called Parenting
ISBN 1-58919-995-2
Copyright © 2001 by Gwendolyn Mitchell Diaz

Published by RiverOak Publishing
P.O. Box 700143
Tulsa, Oklahoma 74170-0143

To my own mother whose prayers have kept me
from places I did not belong and taken me to places
I do not deserve!

Acknowledgments

Thank you, Ed, for your encouragement—and hands-on help with the laundry! Without your support I would never have found the time to complete this manuscript. Zach, MattE., Ben, and Jonathan—without you, life would be so empty. You fill every day with laughter, life, and love. To my two daughters-in-law, Heather and Leslee, thanks for adding beauty to our lives in every way. And, last but not least, to Linda, Jessica, Cindy, Susie, and all my sisters at W.O.W.—your prayers and love kept me going.

Foreword

Motherhood is serious business—whether you're paid in sticky kisses or company stock, whether you're a happily married mom in an old-fashioned nuclear home or a single parent. It's a great privilege to be a mother—but also a big responsibility. And we need to handle it as purposefully as we do career success, because home is where success really matters.

With inspiration and down-to-earth humor, Gwen Diaz reminds us that the countless mundane tasks we perform day after day are critically important to the development of the kids we care so much about. On the days when we feel like we're in over our heads, Gwen helps us remember the pivotal role we play in nurturing our family members; helping them connect in meaningful ways with each other, with the outside world, and—perhaps most important—with their own talents, skills, and spirits, so they become the persons God created them to be. In *Mighty Mom's Secrets for Raising Super Kids*, you'll find plenty of fresh ideas about how to create an atmosphere where your family can enjoy living, laughing, and learning together—and discover how to make lighthearted work of this serious business called motherhood.

Kathy Peel
President, Family Manager Inc.

If you bungle raising your children, I don't think whatever else you do well matters very much.

—Jacqueline Kennedy Onassis

Table of Contents

Introduction

I May Not Be an Expert, but I Am Experienced!

Parents have become so convinced that educators know what is best for children that they forget that they themselves are really the experts.

—Marion Wright Edelman

Almost sixteen years ago, I found myself sitting in the middle of the living room floor surrounded by moving boxes, misplaced furniture, and four hungry children. It was the day after we moved to Lakeland, Florida, and my husband was already on his way to speak at a conference out of town. I was overwhelmed with memories of the friends we had left behind, the melancholy of being in an unfamiliar home in a new city, and the muddle of the recent move.

To make matters worse, each of the four little boys surrounding me were struggling with emotions and feelings of their own—particularly those associated with hunger and tiredness! My five-year-old, unaccustomed to being cooped up in a house, was wired for action. Far too many volts were running through his system, and I couldn't seem to locate the "off" switch. He had confiscated the pillows and cushions from every piece of unloaded furniture and constructed a trampoline in the middle of the floor. After teaching his three-year-old brother to do cartwheels, somersaults, and high dives off the barstools onto the pile of pillows, he invented a new game called "King of the Hill." Brute force established his right to rule over his little brother, and his reign was rapidly becoming a reign of terror.

The baby needed changing and was desperate to be fed, and on top of everything else, my seven-year-old was as sick as a dog. He began puking into a big yellow bowl in the corner of the room.

At that point, I fell apart and started to sob. How could God do this to me? I had never even wanted children in the first place, yet *He* had chosen to give them to me. Not just one or two. Four of them. And all boys!

Besides, I had never wanted to move to Florida. I had been perfectly happy in Georgia, and even in Oregon, before this. Yet, here I was in central Florida in the middle of a hot summer with no shade trees. No icemaker in the fridge. And no friends.

My thoughts continued to spiral downward. I looked around and wondered what on earth had become of my blossoming career. I was an Ivy League graduate who once sat across a table from the top educators in the nation, debating drug education and health issues. Now all I ever sat across the table from were grody little boys slurping big bowls of Cheerios and digging into little boxes of raisins. I spent most of my time in the backyard playing baseball and wiping snotty noses. I hadn't participated in an intellectual conversation in months, and the only book I had read in the last four weeks was *Big Dog, Little Dog* . . . about a thousand times!

Obviously, I was in the wrong place, at the wrong time, surrounded by all the wrong-sized people. God must have made a mistake! He surely didn't mean for me to be trapped in this situation.

Just then, the phone rang.

"I'm calling to see how you are." The annoyingly chipper voice on the other end of the line belonged to one of the few people I had met in town. "I know you must be under the pile with all those kids and a new house and everything a mess. Why don't I get you a baby-sitter, and we'll go play some tennis. You could use a break."

Boy, was she right. "Great!" I jumped at the opportunity. "Give me a few seconds to find the box with my tennis gear and I'll be ready."

As I hung up the phone, my sick seven-year-old laid his head in my lap. The baby crawled over him to get into my arms, and my three-year-old and five-year-old both quit bouncing long enough to notice the tears that were still in my eyes.

"Is Mommy okay? Don't cry, Mommy. We'll help you unpack."

Suddenly, as if lightning had struck the room, a revelation hit me. Either I had to completely change my concept of God—the One whom I taught my children to believe in . . . the One whom I always insisted loves us incredibly . . . the One who knows everything we ever do and can fix anything imaginable—or I had to get my act together and accept the fact that He had placed me in this situation for some awesome, divine reason.

I knew in my heart that God hadn't goofed things up. No mistakes had been made on His part. This had to be exactly where He wanted me to be, at exactly the right time in my life. That meant that I was surrounded by exactly the right-sized people, reading exactly the right books, and participating in exactly the right activities.

For the first time, I began to really understand that there was far more to life than my comfortable surroundings, my college degrees, or my intellectual friends. I didn't need those things to escape the sometimes-frustrating situations I found myself in as a mom. Instead, I needed to learn to enjoy motherhood and find a peaceful fulfillment in it. I needed to choose to be content.

I kissed my feverish child on the forehead, pulled the baby to my breast, and broke into laughter at the contorted faces my three-year-old and five-year-old were making to try and force me to smile.

I called my friend and said, "I don't know what I was thinking, but we're far too busy and having far too much fun around here for me to leave right now."

We filled some bowls with Cheerios, opened some boxes of raisins, and had a picnic amidst the pillows in the middle of the living room floor. Then, we draped sheets and blankets over the chairs to form a big tent, restacked the pillows and cushions underneath, and all took a much-needed nap.

That day mothering took on a whole new perspective for me—one that I want to share with you. I discovered that motherhood was meant to be a blast. And it can be—no matter how difficult the situation. I learned that being able to enjoy and find fulfillment in motherhood is all a matter of understanding and accepting our true priorities and refocusing our efforts with a proper perspective.

I have discovered several "secrets" along the way that have helped me immensely. Some of them were learned through experiences previously shared in *The Adventures of*

Mighty Mom. I hope you don't mind me repeating a few of them. The principles they birthed gave me the confidence to joyfully survive this wonderful odyssey known as motherhood. They have provided me with a framework for finding fulfillment and a reason for wearing a smile. I'd like to share my discoveries with you.

Chapter One

Congratulations, You're a Mother! So Am I!

The future destiny of a child is the work of a mother.

—Napoleon Bonaparte

Timothy and Tomothy were twins. They were the most undemanding, best-behaved, perfectly compliant little boys in the whole world. Their bright blue eyes sparkled in the sunlight, and they wore constant smiles on their dimpled little faces. They were adorable, adaptable, and accommodating. And best of all—they were mine.

Timothy sat still whenever I left him alone in his carriage—even if it was overnight. Tomothy never complained when I forgot to take him along on vacation. Neither of them hollered or ran away from me when I wanted to change their clothes. Neither refused to go to bed when it was past their bedtime. Never once did they bicker or brawl. They were always perfect little gentlemen.

Timothy and Tomothy were my very favorite dolls—ragtag, cuddly, little hand-me-downs from a cousin who had outgrown them several years before. They were my introduction to motherhood. Unfortunately, however, everything I learned about motherhood from that five-year-old experience with Timothy and Tomothy was nullified twenty years later when a real live baby entered my life, screaming at the top of his lungs!

Motherhood isn't exactly what I had envisioned as a little girl. I quickly discovered that real babies don't like to be left out in the rain or stuffed into a suitcase. They don't always stay right where you put them or sleep through the night. Just two days into my role as a mom, I remember staring at my real-life baby with a mixture of awe and terror and commenting to my husband, "I guess we'd better figure out what this parenting thing is all about. I don't think we're allowed to give him back!"

Part of my problem was that the kid didn't come with a manual. I still don't quite understand this. When they send you home from the hardware store with a new lawn mower, they always have the decency to pack in a set of instructions. When they ship you a computer, it usually comes with a technical support number to call for advice and an address to ship it back to when things go very wrong. Babies come with nothing!

Oh sure, the pediatrician gave me a list of shots my baby needed, and the nurse handed me a pamphlet telling me when to start feeding him oatmeal and what to do if he caught a cold or swallowed a marble. But I didn't have a clue what owning a baby was really all about. And to tell the truth, I'm still learning.

I've discovered that motherhood is far different than it was in those "dolly days" when bathing and burping were playtime activities and babies didn't cry—even if they fell out of their carriages. I've realized that motherhood doesn't come equipped with most of the amenities I daydreamed about during high school English classes. There is no huge white mansion equipped with all the latest gizmos and gadgets for entertaining and supervising youngsters, replete with a husband whose only desire is to serve. And motherhood isn't anything like the roles I observed on TV soap operas during my college days. There are no nannies or nurses to handle the details while I pursue an exciting, exotic career.

Let's face facts. I was not prepared to be a mom. Were you? Did you have a clue that newborns like to eat every two hours? Or that sometimes you'd have to do gross things like suck snot from their noses with little bulbous syringes?

No one taught you how to buy groceries or do the dishes or vacuum the house with only one arm, did they? Did anyone happen to mention that it might be wise to lift weights while you were pregnant so that your other arm would be strong enough to lug around a twenty-pound baby while you accomplished the aforementioned tasks? And who clued you in about discipline? Most of us are totally naive when it comes to figuring out what punishments to attach to which crimes.

Several years ago, my five-year-old son and I were having a rough morning. Everything he wanted to do seemed to fit well within my category of unacceptable behavior, and everything I wanted him to do fit easily into his description of unreasonable demands. At one point, I reminded him that he had to wash his hands before he could eat his snack. He decided to debate the issue, but after a while I insisted that we were not going to discuss it any further. If he refused to obey me one more time, he would not get a snack at all.

I was feeding an infant in a high chair and supervising a toddler with finger paints, so my back was turned to my five-year-old during much of the discussion. Having made my final point, I turned to gauge his response. There he stood in the middle of the kitchen floor—with his tongue sticking straight out at me!

I felt absolutely and completely devastated. How could my wonderful child do that to anyone, let alone *me*—his own *mother?* The one who had just made him his very own Superman cape . . . the one who snuck out with him after dark to play flashlight tag . . . the one who sometimes put blue food coloring in his ice cream so that it would look like the ice cream he saw on cartoons?

I had no clue how to respond.

Sensing my shock and utter dismay, he quickly approached and gave me a big hug. "Oh, Mommy," he looked up at me with his huge brown eyes. "I wasn't sticking my tongue out at you. I was sticking it out at the wall. You just got in the way!"

I was totally unprepared to handle the situation. Was I supposed to smack him on the bottom for lying? Wash his mouth out with soap? Send him to bed for the duration of the day? Maybe I should have stood him in the corner and made him stick his tongue out at the wall for ten more minutes. That would certainly have taught him a lesson. Or would it?

I still don't know exactly how I should have reacted that morning. I do know for certain that collapsing on the floor in a fit of hysterical laughter was definitely not an acceptable response. But I couldn't help it. For some reason, my utter incompetence in the face of his ingenuity cracked me up. So I just sat on the floor and laughed, while he ran to the sink and washed his hands. Still giggling, I gave him his snack. Then, for weeks I worried that my warped sense of humor might someday lead my child into a life of juvenile delinquency.

I've always marveled at the fact that motherhood is one of the most difficult jobs to accomplish, yet it is one of the easiest to secure. Application requirements don't exist. There are no educational, financial, or marital constraints. Rarely does anyone perform a background check or conduct a psychological evaluation. One needs no previous experience to qualify. The only discriminating factor in the whole process is gender. Motherhood is one of the few jobs remaining that discriminates according to sex. But other than the fact that we are required to be female, no one prescreens us for our capabilities. No one hands us a "how-to" manual. And seldom does anyone pass out trophies for our accomplishments.

It is quite surprising how many children survive in spite of their mothers.

—Norman Douglas

To put it bluntly, motherhood is an around-the-clock occupation without a defined job description, a full-time challenge without much support, a permanent position without the promise of compensation. And, although the mantle of motherhood may not be exactly what we anticipated or desired or were prepared for, once a child enters our home, the title of "Mother" is permanently attached to our resume´.

So, how do we successfully accomplish this task?

Jeff Siemon, a friend of mine, played linebacker for the Minnesota Vikings during the 1970s and '80s. He relayed to me a story that his head coach, Bud Grant, would often tell to inspire his players when they faced a difficult situation. It's about a project that our government undertook during the Cold War of the 1960s.

The United States decided to build a radar system in the Northwest Territories of Canada that would detect any movement by the Russians toward the North American continent. However, it seems the Cold War got its name for more than one reason. The military personnel found it very difficult to work in the bitter, 50-degrees-below-zero temperatures that they encountered. The GIs could only bear to work outdoors in the howling wind and inhumane weather for a few minutes at a time. So, they had to work in shifts. No more than twenty or thirty minutes after going out, each shift would have to rush back inside to warm up. By then their eyelids had frozen open, and they were in constant fear of frostbite and hypothermia.

Noticing that native Eskimos could labor outdoors for many hours at a time without much difficulty, government officials decided to train them to work on the project, even though they lacked the experience and expertise of the GIs. Sure enough, they found an excellent workforce that was able to operate the bulldozers and other machinery successfully, even in the harsh, inhumane environment— sometimes staying outside for an entire workday.

"How do they do that?" the government wanted to know. "How do they stay out there for so long in subzero temperatures without freezing to death? And why can't our guys do the same?"

So, they conducted tests, spending millions of dollars to determine what biological differences made the native Eskimos so much more suitable to working in extremely cold environments than the GIs from the "lower forty-eight." They did all kinds of blood tests, fat tests, and muscle tests, but they could find no distinguishing characteristics.

In their final conclusion, the only difference the government could find between the two groups of men was in their psychological approach to the challenging situation. You see, when the GIs went outside, their main goal was to stay warm. The Eskimos, on the other hand, went outdoors with the goal of accomplishing a task. They anticipated that they would get cold, and they knew that they would remain cold for quite a while. But they allowed their bodies to adjust, and they committed themselves to endure until they were finished. While the GIs were hung up on the circumstances, the Eskimos were focused on the job at hand. Not only did they adapt and endure—they excelled at what they did.

How well we do as moms has nothing to do with our past experience, our previous expectations, or our present expertise. It has to do with our willingness to adjust and our commitment to endure and excel. The goal of motherhood should not be to merely survive each obstacle that comes along. Our expectations as mothers should be that we will thrive over the long haul and, therefore, our kids will too! We must accept motherhood as the awesome responsibility it was created to be. Sure, there will be times when we'll blow it. But being a mom can be a joyous journey filled with wonder and excitement, satisfaction and delight. Motherhood can, and must be, a task at which we excel. Hang in there!

✿ How well prepared was I to become a mother? In what areas do I wish I had been better prepared?

✿ What one aspect of mothering do I need to embrace more? In what area does God want me to thrive, rather than just survive?

A Mother's Prayer

*Help me, Lord, I'm a mom! Make me the mother
You want me to be. I am only beginning to
understand the vital importance of my role. Please
help me not take my responsibilities for granted.
Place within me a desire to adapt, a commitment to
endure, and the ability to excel. Give me a
dedicated heart, dear God, one that embraces all
You intended motherhood to be.*

Chapter Two

Motherhood Is an Awesome Assignment with Lots of "Home" Work

*Our children are not just going to be
'our children' – they are going to be other
people's husbands and wives and the parents
of our grandchildren.*

—Mary S. Calderone

It was a Tuesday evening. Our high school baseball team had just won a huge game, and we were all going nuts. Whooping and hollering, everyone on the team swarmed the field and began giving each other "high fives." Everyone, that is, except my fifteen-year-old.

I couldn't figure out Ben's lack of enthusiasm. He's usually so animated. But when I spotted him, he had a puzzled, almost dejected look on his face. Instead of running to greet me, he sauntered over, as though he'd lost his best friend.

"What's the matter, Ben? I asked. "Why aren't you excited? Your team just won a huge game!"

"Yeah, but I think I probably failed my Life Skills class," he mumbled dejectedly. "I left my stupid 'egg babies' home without a baby-sitter!"

I didn't have a clue what he was talking about. I wondered if the hit that he had taken when he slid into second base had somehow scrambled his brains.

"What on earth is an 'egg baby'?" I wanted to know.

On the way home, Ben filled me in. At school that day, each student had been given an egg. For three days, they had to pretend it was a real child. They were to treat "their baby" gently and take it with them wherever they went. The exercise was designed to be a lesson in the realities and responsibilities of becoming a parent. Grades would depend on how carefully and completely the students cared for their eggs.

Each egg came with a little felt cap and a silly felt-tip pen smile. Ben, much to his chagrin, had been given the only set of "twins." Actually, I think the teacher had an extra egg left over and figured Ben could use a spare.

Ben managed to transport his "egg babies" home in his backpack without cracking them. But once he arrived, he immediately shoved them in the fridge.

The last place he had ever expected to run into his teacher was at the ball field that night. But there she was! And, sure enough, sometime during the sixth inning she managed to ask him through the dugout fence where his "egg twins" were. She let him know in no uncertain terms that "Home, chillin' in the fridge" was not an acceptable answer.

"You didn't *really* expect me to bring *eggs* with *faces* on them to the *ball field*, did you?" he asked incredulously. "Besides, they're a whole lot safer in the fridge than they would be out here. Do you know what a foul ball can do to an egg?"

His teacher wasn't the least bit amused by his logic. "It's considered child abuse to leave your babies unattended," she answered. "I'll have to mark your grade way down."

"Child abuse! That's ridiculous!" He responded, more than a little perturbed. "Anyway, I didn't leave them home unattended. The cat is taking care of them."

"I'm afraid cats can't function as baby-sitters," she said, shaking her head.

"Hey, if eggs can be babies, why can't cats be baby-sitters?"

His argument was clever, but she didn't buy it.

Consequently, those "egg babies" got shoved into a shoebox stuffed with Easter grass, crammed into his backpack, and carried around with him for the better part of two days in an effort to salvage his grade.

"Egg kids are a real pain," he grumbled quite often. "You can't just dump them somewhere. You've got to drag them with you wherever you go."

Ben was thrilled when Thursday finally rolled around. With much relief, he turned his "egg babies" back over to his teacher's care. They both stank a little. I'm sure he never gave them baths. And one baby had somehow cracked its skull in the shoebox. (Fortunately it was hard-boiled.) But, somehow he managed to survive and get a passing grade.

I applaud that teacher's assignment. I think everyone should be given such a responsibility prior to parenthood. There's a lot to be learned from carrying "egg babies" around for a week!

We would never think of giving our students a calculus assignment if they had not previously studied high school algebra. To ask a child to conjugate a verb before that child learned his parts of speech would be just as ridiculous. Yet, very few of us go through a learning process that prepares us for raising children. Even so, once a child enters our home, we cannot back out of the assignment—no matter how ill prepared we may be.

Yes, motherhood is an assignment—the most important, most awesome assignment we will ever receive. Just like Ben's "egg baby" venture, during the twenty or so years it takes us to complete that assignment, our efforts are continually being evaluated. Did you realize that? We actually receive grades for our efforts as moms! Scary thought, isn't it?

Of course our grades aren't announced as numbers or letters. Our accomplishments are posted in other forms. They might appear as a note sent home by a teacher that indicates an area of concern—or as an award from an employer that highlights values we have instilled. They might be revealed in a kind deed our child does for a neighbor—or their acquisition of an unhealthy habit. They could show up in our child's response to a challenge or his ability to adapt to a new situation. Sometimes they astonish us in the appearance of a scholarship or startle us in the form of a police report. Whatever appearance the evaluations take, our efforts to complete our assignment do not go unnoticed nor remain ungraded.

When Matthew was three, my husband and I decided that he should attend nursery school a couple of mornings a week. Several of Matthew's friends attended the school, and he didn't want to be left out. We saw it as a great opportunity for me to spend some time alone with his one-year-old baby brother—and to get the grocery shopping done!

On just his second morning there, Matthew's teacher pulled me aside as I picked him up after school. "Matthew has developed a tremendous sense of right and wrong," she started to explain.

I beamed. I had obviously taught my son well.

"But," she continued, "he seems to think that it is his job to force that understanding on everyone else."

Uh-oh. Obviously, several lessons remained in the "Teaching One's Child How to Decipher Right from Wrong" chapter of my mothering assignment.

Matthew's teacher explained that she had gone over the playground rules with her class that morning. She had stressed to the children that they should not walk in front of the swings and that they should never climb up the slide the wrong way. However, one little boy insisted on disobeying. He kept running in front of the swings, and the teacher kept grabbing him and pulling him aside. Finally, the teacher positioned herself where he could no longer get near the swing set without passing her. Immediately, the boy turned around and darted up the slide—the wrong way, of course.

Matthew had evidently been observing all this. He realized that the teacher was exhausted and unable to catch the naughty little boy, so he took it upon himself to enforce the rules for her. He grabbed the boy by the shoe, yanked him down the slide, and threw him to the ground. "Don't you neva, eva disobey da teacha again!" he commanded, standing over the frightened child.

"Although I appreciated his assistance very much at the moment," his teacher remarked, "he must be taught that he is only responsible for his own behavior, not the behavior of others." She explained how both boys had been sent inside for the remainder of playtime. "By the way," she added with a smile, "the other little boy didn't disobey me the rest of the day."

Matthew and I went to work right away on the next step in his "deciphering right and wrong" lesson. It was a tough lesson for him to comprehend, since he had a strong desire for justice and a limited understanding of mercy. As a matter of fact, twenty years later, we're still working on it!

Everybody knows how to raise children, except the people who have them.

—P.J. O'Rourke

One of the biggest difficulties we face in fulfilling our assignments as mothers relates to the fact that the role of Mom and the status of families are undergoing constant revision in our society. This constant state of change leaves many of us struggling to decipher exactly what tasks and responsibilities really belong to us.

Erma Bombeck, whose wit and wisdom filled our newspapers from 1965 until 1996, once described motherhood as an exercise in flying kites. Our children are the kites. "You spend a lifetime trying to get them off the ground," she wrote. "You run with them until you're both

breathless . . . they crash . . . you add a longer tail . . . they
hit the rooftop . . . you pluck them out of the spout. You
patch and comfort, adjust and teach. You watch them lifted
by the wind and assure them that someday they'll fly."[1]

Shortly after Erma wrote that description, I made a
startling discovery. Most of my friends had never flown kites
with their children! Therefore, they didn't have a clue what
Erma was talking about. Sadly, many moms don't make time
for such "frivolous" activities with their children. They
seldom walk with their kids, let alone run with them or
watch them fly kites. It's too easy to get caught up doing
other more "important" things.

Allegorically speaking, many of my friends drop their kids
off at the kite-flying fields of life and hand the strings over to
someone else to get them off the ground. Few moms stick
around to teach their children to fly. Even fewer are there to
pluck the damaged ones off the rooftops or out of the spouts.
Often, they don't even know that their children are in the
gutter until they stumble over a bedraggled one, covered with
leaves and muck and clogging up the flow of life. Then, they
haul him off to a so-called "expert," hoping to get him all
patched up, readjusted, and ready to try to fly on his own
again.

Old-fashioned motherhood used to necessitate many
precious hours spent with a child, providing task training and

lessons in life management skills. Mothers were the ones who encouraged the blossoming of talents and helped hone the individual skills of their children. They worked diligently to instill manners and mold personalities. It was a mother's role to ensure that the children who left her home were capable of running a household of their own. Parenting required a lot of action, interaction, and close proximity before a child reached adulthood—and before a mother could cut the strings and let her kite fly free.

But, so often now, mothers are no longer the primary caregivers or the chief trainers in their children's lives. Like some of my friends, many moms have become merely the organizers and facilitators of a multitude of activities. They substitute activities for attendance in the lives of their children. They are great with calendars and schedules, but few take the time to actually help their children conjugate verbs or calculate the area of an isosceles triangle. (Oops! I couldn't even begin to spell "isosceles" without the aid of my spell-check button!)

Few moms teach their children how to iron their own clothes or sew on buttons or plant shrubs in the backyard. The training roles traditionally assigned to mothers have been meted out to other caregivers: teachers, coaches, church staff, and even peers. The fact that one teacher took time out of my sixth-grade child's science class to teach conflict resolution and that fifth graders are being taught courses in human sexuality tells me that educators do not feel that we are accomplishing all that we should be in our homes.

It is sad to say, but "mother" is no longer an action verb. The word has become nothing more than a proper noun as we have appointed our tasks to others and ultimately allowed them to usurp our position. We have relinquished our role of leadership and given strangers the authority to inform us concerning what is right and wrong for our children, what is acceptable or unacceptable in our homes, what is to be tolerated and what is to be deplored in our lives.

Yes, mothers once held the single most vital position in society. It was our job to teach the next generation how to determine right from wrong, to instruct them in making sound judgments and morally acceptable decisions, to train them to live at peace in the world. But we have gradually allowed ourselves to be replaced by a myriad of other faces and factors. And, unfortunately, our replacements are not always doing very well!

One of the biggest changes in the role and duties of motherhood came about as many of us entered the work-force. For several years, it was necessary for me to go to work outside our home to help provide for the needs of my family.

My husband was in graduate school for four of those years. Then when he graduated, we found ourselves in a new situation in a new town. The company he worked for was not established enough at the time to pay him a salary that met our needs. If I had not continued to work, we would have had to give up housing or food or his new career. None of these options seemed too appealing. But as my husband's expertise and income increased at work, and the number of children increased in our home, we felt it was best for me to be with them as much as possible. I gave up my career and became a work-at-home mom. The decision was a tough one—but oh, so right for us!

However, as my children approached adolescence, I began to feel the necessity of adding more income to the family. I reasoned that I needed to provide for the additional needs of my growing children. An honest self-evaluation several months into the process, though, caused me to admit that I was not actually using this income to *provide* for my kids. No, I was using it to *pamper* them (and myself—just a little!). I realized in theory that there was a huge difference between "providing" and "pampering," but, in reality, I failed to distinguish the difference for quite a while.

I discovered that *"providing"* is making sure that my children have a roof over their heads, clean sheets on their beds, a change of clothes for school, food on their plates, and something to play with besides dirt. *"Pampering"* is providing that roof over their heads—plus a designer spaceship wallpaper border across the top of their bedroom walls. It is tucking them in at night under official NFL sheets from the JC Penney catalog, dressing them in the very latest (and fleeting) fads in the world of children's fashion, eating out at fancy burger joints, and buying a trampoline for the backyard.

I'm not saying that pampering my children was wrong or bad—it just was not *necessary*. I realized that my kids could grow up just fine without any of the "extras" my income provided. But they couldn't grow up as well as they should without my consistent love and attention. *"Pampering"* was keeping me from carrying out many of my important assignments as a mother.

I have a friend who works as a builder. He insists that he can build a very adequate house in the area where we live—with three bedrooms and a bath, a great room, and a fully appointed kitchen, even another half-bath if necessary—for around $60,000! He doesn't build any, though, because nobody will buy them anymore. Young couples these days aren't willing to start at the same lowly point that their parents did twenty or thirty years ago. So, they start their married lives and their families already in debt. And since they often aren't willing to sacrifice any of the luxuries they've grown accustomed to, the moms must go to work. Instead of sacrificing the luxuries, they sacrifice their children.

There are legitimate reasons for working outside the home. That's okay—as long as we keep our priorities in the right order. Our children must always come first. But we need to be willing to reevaluate our situations every once in a while. *"I've got to work in order to provide for my kids' needs"* often isn't the most honest assessment.

If we aren't careful, we will miss out on the butterfly catching, kite flying, and star counting moments in our children's lives. What is a pampered lifestyle worth, compared to the joy of sharing these experiences with our children? No matter how exhausted or overwhelmed we may become in the less-than-glamorous, day-to-day events of mothering—childhood is all too fleeting. Before we know it, our "kites" will be gone.

I admit that, on the surface, motherhood is not the most enticing job opportunity available. It's only natural to prefer "finding oneself" to searching for the missing, grungy tennis shoes that inevitably wind up stuffed in some obscure spot, like the drawer underneath the oven or the recycling bin. Reaching for the stars in a rewarding career is much more stimulating than straining to retrieve the last box of baby wipes from the top of a grocery store shelf.

Dreaming about travelling to Europe and viewing Paris from the top of the Eiffel Tower is far more pleasant than actually chaperoning a bunch of first graders on a field trip to the fire station.

But when we have a child, our one calling in life—above all others—becomes the mothering of that child to maturity and independence. Anything else we choose to participate in—careers, clubs, service organizations, tennis lessons, exercise classes, and the like—must only be undertaken if they can help us fulfill our primary role. If any activity gets in the way of mothering, we should get rid of it. We must not try to fit our kids into our lives and our schedules. Instead we must design our lives and schedules to fit around our kids. The privilege of parenting real children (and not just "egg babies") is the most awesome assignment we will ever receive! And an A+ at the end of the term will make every ounce of energy we put into our "home" work well worth the effort.

✿ What letter grade does my "mothering" deserve so far?
✿ What grade do I think my child would give me? Am I brave enough to ask?
✿ When was the last time I *trained* my child to do something? What was it?

A Mother's Prayer

Teach me, Lord, to be a good mother. Please help
me to grasp the scope of my responsibility—the
awesomeness of my role. Remind me when I get
weary that this is the most important assignment
I will ever receive. Let my "grades" reflect an
honest, whole-hearted effort to be the mother You
want me to be. Please give me a diligent heart,
dear God, so that, with Your help, my children
will prosper.

Chapter Three

If We Don't Plan Where Our Kids Are Going, Chances Are They'll Wind Up Someplace Else

One day Alice came to a fork in the road
and saw a Cheshire cat in a tree.

"Which road do I take?" she asked.

"Where do you want to go?" was his response.

"I don't know," Alice answered.

"Then," said the cat, "it doesn't matter."

—Lewis Carroll (*Alice in Wonderland*)

My five-year-old son was angry—very angry. Ben was adamantly opposed to the sentence I had just imposed on him. He insisted that twenty minutes under house arrest was far too stiff a penalty. After all, his only crime was kicking his brother's soccer ball into the pond—for the third time! He obstinately informed me of my injustice all the way to his bedroom. In order to prove how grossly unfair I had been in assessing his punishment, he decided to run away.

A few minutes after I closed the door to his room, Ben dumped out the contents of his backpack, spewing tattered papers and broken crayons all over his bed. He reloaded it with two pairs of underwear, a jacket, a toothbrush, and his favorite remote-controlled car. He finished his packing just about the time the kitchen timer buzzed to signal his release. But he continued with his escape plan. Sneaking out of his bedroom, he tiptoed down the hallway and quietly let himself out the backdoor.

I watched him go. I peeked out of the bathroom window just in time to see him crawl stealthily around the side of the house then dart down to the sidewalk. I got a little nervous as he headed up the street toward the main road. As I ran out the front door to stop him, he hesitated. A large neighborhood dog was paying him a visit. He backed up slowly, turned around, and then quickly made his way back toward our house. I scooted inside without being noticed and kept an eye on him through the living room window. My little runaway wandered back and forth aimlessly in front of the house for nearly half an hour, finally plopping himself down on a pile of logs just a few feet from our mailbox. For about ten minutes, he vented his anger by kicking the bark off a stump. Then, he headed back into the house.

"Where have you been?" I asked, trying to appear nonchalant. "I was getting worried about you."

"I ran far away," Ben replied. His green eyes flashed with defiance as he stared up at me.

I wasn't at all sure how to handle the situation, so I thought I'd give him an opportunity to express his feelings. "Did you have fun where you went?"

"Well, I didn't quite get all the way to where I was going." His answer now sounded a little more thoughtful and, perhaps, a little less rebellious.

"Why not?" I wondered aloud, still not quite sure where to go with this current state of affairs.

There was a long pause. Then, Ben took a deep breath. "I guess because I wasn't really sure where I wanted to be." He turned and ran outside to play with his brothers before I could mete out any further punishment for having jumped jail.

I know that my son learned a lesson that day about the foolishness of kicking his brother's soccer ball into the lake—he didn't do it again for at least a week. But, hopefully, he also learned a more important lesson about the futility of leaping headlong into a situation without a plan or goal in mind. Ben didn't have a clue where he was going that afternoon when he headed out the door. Consequently he didn't get anywhere.

Often we enter motherhood the same way Ben entered the big "outside" world. We jump into the role with all kinds of enthusiasm. We can't wait to have a baby! However, when that baby arrives, we don't have a plan as to where to go from there. We don't have a clue how we're going to get that child to sleep through the night or eat his green beans, let alone how we're going to train him to assume a productive role in society. About the time our baby has outgrown the shower gifts we received, we find ourselves winging it. We resign ourselves to playing our mothering role by ear, just trying to survive one day at a time.

The thought is a sad one, but I dare say that few of us plan the progression and outcome of our parenting duties half as carefully as we planned our first prom date or the redecoration of our master bedroom.

Before we had children of our own, my husband and I found ourselves teaching a class in a Learning Center with another couple. For two-and-a-half hours each Sunday, we were responsible for about fifty energetic six, seven, and eight-year-olds while their parents attended the church service and fellowship hour. At the beginning of each week, we met for dinner with the other couple to plan our lessons and design complementary activities. These sessions sometimes lasted more than three hours, since we had to formulate goals and objectives, prepare teaching agendas, and create evaluation techniques. Before we left that evening, we had planned creative ways to teach the lesson, music to enhance it, crafts to reinforce it, playtime activities to wear the kids out, and snacks to jazz them back up. Every last second of that two-and-a-half hours was accounted for. But that was just the beginning. Once the lessons were planned, it was my job to gather the materials necessary for the lesson, create sample crafts, gather equipment for the playtime activities, and purchase the snacks. Thankfully, someone else did the music!

Later in the week, we got together to be sure we had our materials and our act together. Hours of planning and preparation went into every single lesson, every single week, for over two years. All this so we could teach and transform someone else's kids.

Several years of mothering transpired before I realized that my life revealed a huge dichotomy. When I had been in charge of training someone else's children, I spared no amount of time or effort. However, I put very little planning or preparation time into the teaching and transforming of my own kids.

Without realizing it, I had developed the attitude, "If I can just hang in there long enough, my job will eventually be over—by default if nothing else!" I figured that, sooner or later, my kids would grow up and leave home and, hopefully, things wouldn't get too goofed up in the process. I guess I planned to judge my parenting efforts as adequate if I could one day look around and discover that each of my children had successfully flown the coop. "*Somehow*," I reasoned, "they'll inevitably make it to adulthood. *Someway* they'll mature and make a contribution to society. *Someday* I will have completed my task."

But when I took the time to notice, I realized that the "*somehow, someway, someday*" attitude I had maintained was not working in our society. This attitude was encouraging many kids to become involved in drugs, drinking, and other dangerous escapades. This attitude was getting them blown apart by angry classmates at school.

> *"Just so long as I get somewhere,"* Alice added as an explanation. *"Oh, you're sure to do that,"* said the Cat, *"if you only walk long enough."*
>
> —Lewis Carroll
> (*Alice in Wonderland*)

I had an epiphany when I discovered that King Solomon, in Psalm 127, describes our children as arrows in the hands of a young warrior. I realized that young warriors trained diligently to use their weapons. They never haphazardly discharged their arrows or let them fly aimlessly across an open meadow. They launched them with strength and precision, directly at a particular target. And, once the arrows were released from the hands of a young warrior, they were expected to hit their mark.

Hmmm, I reflected, *So that's how I'm supposed to view my children . . . as arrows! They are designed to have direction and purpose, and they're supposed to carry with them the possibility of making an impact and a difference.*

Wow! I was just kind of carrying mine around in my quiver, hoping that one day they'd grow out of it and find a quiver of their own. Instead, I should have been molding my children's characters. I needed to assist them in accomplishing certain objectives before I ever allowed them to leave my home and my sphere of influence. For the first time, I began to establish real goals for my mothering.

It quickly became obvious that the goals I needed to set for my children should cultivate their character rather than push them toward a particular career. I did not want to corner my youngsters into cozy, little niches of my own design. Too many parents create boxes, then try to force their children to fit inside them. But those ill-fitting boxes hurt their kids' hearts just as much as an ill-fitting pair of shoes would hurt their feet. Such stifled children sometimes end up with emotional blisters that eventually make it hard for them to walk or even stand up on their own.

I decided to cherish principles, moral fiber, and integrity above grades, athletic prowess, and tidy bedrooms.

To avoid establishing goals that were too restrictive or confining, I asked myself this question: *Can my child either be a sitting judge or a standup comedian; a famous surgeon or a faithful garbage collector; an investment analyst or a lawn care specialist— and still achieve the goals I have set for him?* If I answered yes, then my goals were probably fair and my box was probably not too small.

I decided to accomplish my goal-setting by listing three to five qualities that I wanted to see emerge as distinguishing characteristics in each child's life by the time he left home. I knew I couldn't handle many more than that! I included traits such as honesty, generosity, commitment to family, contentment, and the ability to function independently. They varied depending on the personality of each child and changed somewhat over time—depending sometimes on my maturation as a mom.

Fathers and mothers have lost the idea that the highest aspiration they might have for their children is for them to be wise . . . specialized competence and success are all that they can imagine.

—Allan Bloom (*The Closing of the American Mind*)

Beside these positive characteristics, I listed three to five qualities that I refused to tolerate in each child's life. These included traits such as deceitfulness, self-centeredness, jealousy, and pessimism—which often takes the form of whining!

Completing this exercise provided definitive direction and purpose for my mothering. I found targets to shoot toward. If I noticed the negative traits I had chosen not to tolerate emerging in one of my sons' lives, I knew it was time to intervene. In the absence of the positive traits, I recognized the need for additional training.

With just a few concrete goals in mind, most of the tasks and activities associated with motherhood began to fit into two simple categories: (1) this task or activity helps accomplish my goals or (2) this one does not.

All of a sudden, many of the huge decisions in life became very straightforward! If I discovered that something my children, or I, desired to become involved in would not help to achieve the goals I had set, then there was no reason to waste anyone's time pursuing it.

By approaching life and its plethora of possibilities in this manner, there came a purpose and simplicity to mothering. For example, since a primary goal for my children was for them to be able to function independently when they left my care, it became important for me to train them in the basic duties of household management. In order to be successful in their independence, they had to learn how to shop for their own food and plan decent meals. They needed to learn how to make a budget and handle their own money. They had to learn to keep their rooms somewhat livable and the bathroom semi-sanitary! (Do you realize how many hours go into teaching four male children to lower the potty seat when they are finished using it—especially when their own father is still learning this lesson?) And my sons also needed to begin to learn how to establish their own goals.

When I desired for one child to become more committed to the other members of our family, I had to make sure there was plenty of time available in his schedule for him to attend his brothers' baseball games. Having spare time became more valuable than adding something like drum lessons to his daily agenda. (Of course, the only reason he had the sudden urge to bang on drums was because the neighbor's kids were taking lessons and he was jealous.)

When I knew ahead of time where my kids were headed in life, I could determine which activities would help them get there and which ones would merely get in the way.

There is another very important thing I learned about setting and achieving goals for my family. My own personal behavior had to model the character goals I had established for my children or they would never have reached them. Say, for instance, one of my goals for my children is that they learn to be honest and trustworthy. Then I cannot allow myself to call in sick at work when I am really going to take the family to the beach for the day. I cannot tell my child to inform a telephone caller that I am not home when I am actually engrossed in some other activity. Aiming children toward honesty involves showing them the way.

We must not only establish goals, we must actively steer our children toward them every day. Otherwise, our goals become as useless as an archery target that's left to rot inside a storage shed. Constantly keeping the goals I have set for my children in the front of my mind, and taped the refrigerator door, focuses and simplifies my mothering experiences.

Too many children are wandering around (or sitting around kicking the bark off stumps with their heels like Ben did) without a clue as to where they are headed in life, because mothers like me have never pointed them in any direction. We can't just hang in there, hoping that *somehow, someway, someday* our kids will succeed. We need to start taking our child-raising assignment more seriously—making it our top priority. In order to do this, we need to take time to set character goals for our children.

Then we must strive to reach them. The future of our children is at stake, as well as the well-being of our society. Although our children make up only about one-third of our population, they make up 100 percent of our future!

❀ What five characteristics do I want to distinguish my child's life by the time he leaves home?

❀ How am I going to steer my child toward one of these goals today?

A Mother's Prayer

Help me, Lord, as I aim my children toward important goals. Be my guide as I seek to develop character and personality traits in them that will have lasting significance. When they leave home, may their lives make a difference in their world because of the time and effort I took to train and mold them. Give me a discerning heart, dear God, one that is able to focus on what is significant to You.

Chapter Four

Being Their Mother Is Much More Important than Being Their Friend

Most of all the other beautiful things in life come by twos and threes, by dozens and hundreds. (There are) plenty of roses, stars, sunsets, rainbows, brothers and sisters, aunts and cousins, but (there is) only one mother in the whole world.

—Kate Douglas Wiggen

All the kids said Judy was a great mom. They loved to hang out at her house and shoot hoops, or swim in the pool, or watch TV. She always had plenty of snacks and sodas to drink. Maybe that was it—the sodas—that suddenly made her the most popular mom on the block and designated her house as the "place to be."

I tended to serve things like apples and Tang between scrimmages and skirmishes. Perhaps that was the problem. Kids didn't seem to like healthy food—given any other alternative. I decided to stock a few sodas and some Oreos in the pantry hoping to increase my popularity and lure my kids and their friends back home. My sons were thrilled with the new culinary treats, but their friends didn't seem to hang around any more than they had prior to cookies and carbonation.

I couldn't figure out what made Judy's place so much more attractive than mine. I felt jealous. Until one day one of my children let the comment slip that at Judy's house— yes, all the kids called her by her first name—they were allowed to watch whatever television shows they wanted to. "And, oh yeah," another one added, "we can help ourselves to food and drinks whenever we're hungry or thirsty."

"You mean Mrs. Lewis doesn't have rules about what you can or cannot watch?" I was shocked, realizing how easily pre-pubescent teenagers are lured into watching questionable material.

"No, she's really cool. She trusts us. And lots of times she watches with us. She likes the same kind of stuff we do," one of my older sons replied.

"Yeah, she even laughs when they talk about sex," the youngest one giggled. One of his older brothers smacked him on the head.

That was the last time they hung out at Judy's house, unless I accompanied them. All through high school, Judy's place was the weekend hangout—for kids other than my own. She really "understood" teenagers. She watched less and less TV with them, knowing that if they were overly supervised, they wouldn't hang around as much. She traded sodas for alcohol. She rationalized that if they didn't get it at her house, they would go somewhere else where it might be more dangerous. She sure was popular, but her popularity came with a price as her children found themselves deeply involved in a world of alcohol and drugs. Judy mistook friendship for leadership and popularity for positive parenting.

I can guarantee you one thing right off the bat—if you're a good mom, you won't always be popular. Nobody likes rules, even when they are made for their own good. Few people like fences, even if they are for their own protection. And when you're the one making the rules and mending the fences, chances are there will be times when you are very unpopular.

It's much more fun just to be a friend than a leader. But your children are not in need of more friends. There are many kids their own age from whom they can choose comrades and companions. And often they change their friends as quickly as they change their shoes. But they will only ever have one mother—and that's you! Your job is to provide them with leadership and love—leadership that will guide them along the safe paths in life and love that is far more deep and secure than that of a friend.

There has been a lot of hoopla recently about a premise that peers, more than parents, influence the long-term personality development of a child. This is true only in cases where the parents have given up their roles as leaders and reneged on their responsibility to love their children at all costs. If we are honest, we will all admit that, in our hearts and guts, we know parents are the ones who are largely responsible for how their children turn out. It is up to the parents to orchestrate the effect and outcome of other influencing factors such as peers, school, and neighborhood activities.

I cannot emphasize strongly enough that we, as parents, are supposed to be the leaders. Our leadership must be encompassed with love. Every rule we choose to enforce, every boundary we put in place, every path we choose to lead them down must be done for the good of our children and their future outcome. We must set the direction and help maintain the course that our children take as they approach adulthood. I guarantee you—if we don't, someone else will! If we're fortunate, that someone will be a church youth leader or a schoolteacher. But chances are, it will be a peer group or a boyfriend or girlfriend. And it may even be a drug dealer or a well-meaning neighbor—like Judy—who is out to lunch on her principles and priorities.

Children and teenagers are searching for someone who will care enough to provide them with leadership. Realizing they are under someone's care and tutelage makes them feel worthwhile. It boosts their self-esteem and gives their lives direction. There is no better person to organize and coordinate the making of their future than their own mother.

The love a mother has for her children is far deeper and much more secure than the love that can be offered by a friend. Ross Campbell, in his book *How to Really Love Your Child*, points out that all children come into the world equipped with emotional tanks. Just like the gas tanks in our cars, they need to be constantly refilled in order for everything to run smoothly. The more full their tanks, the more positive their feelings will be and the better they will behave. Dr. Campbell says that a child's behavior is a direct indication of the condition of his tank.[2]

How do we fill our child's emotional tank? One way is through eye contact. Once, when my Matthew was about three years old, I was busy doing the dishes in the kitchen when he pulled a stool up beside me and climbed on top. He grabbed my face in both his hands and in a very serious tone of voice commanded, "Listen to me with your eyes, Mommy. I'm important!" Eye contact is vital if we want to convey our love to our children—and not just when we want to get our point across.

Moms are naturally good at communicating with their eyes. Unfortunately it's usually in a negative context. We have all kinds of famous "mother's looks" that we use to convey our displeasure without saying a word.

For instance, there's the "cut that out—or else" look we use so often. For this one, we cock our heads to one side, peer out of the corners of our eyes, and squint the eye closest to the child who is making gravy rivers in his mashed potatoes at the Country Club buffet. It usually catches his attention enough to motivate him to dam up the dike before the gravy seeps onto the linen tablecloth.

Then there's the glare that translates, "You are really close to being in a huge heap of trouble." For this one, we stare straight at our child with both our eyes half shut and our lips forming a perfectly straight line. This comes in handy when one of our older children is beating up a younger sibling in the checkout lane at the grocery store.

I recently perfected another look where my eyelashes start to flutter, my mouth opens to reveal clenched teeth, and my chest starts to heave. I use it when my sons are griping in the car. It alerts them to the fact that they had better bail out of the car before it comes to a complete halt in the driveway, so they can run for their lives.

No, the kind of eye contact that conveys love and fills the emotional tanks of our children is a doting, smiling, pleasant look—especially at seemingly unimportant or unsolicited times. (This works for people of all ages, I might add.) It communicates unconditional love and admiration and says to them, "You are so neat and special, and I love you from the bottom of my heart, just because you are you!" A child who has plenty of this type of eye contact not only feels loved, he feels worthwhile.

In order to really communicate with kids, we've got to practice deep knee bends. We've got to get down there so we're face-to-face with them.

—Leo Buscaglia

Another important way we must communicate our love and boost our child's self-esteem is through physical touch. Sadly, studies show that most moms seldom touch their children these days except when it is necessary. I know this sounds unbelievable, but it's true. Think about this. Most physical contact comes in the form of aid—helping a child up the steps, or into a car seat, or with the zipper on his jacket. Occasionally there is a kiss that goes along with a Band-

Aid or a hug as a child is helped out of a car and headed into preschool. But by the time a child is self-sufficient enough to dry his own back and buckle his own seat belt, a mother's hand rarely comes in contact with her child's skin. This is not only sad, it is appalling.

We talk poignantly about the aging citizens in our nursing homes and the fact that they receive very little touch. Studies have been done which show how much better the elderly fare emotionally and physically when they receive even a minimum of corporeal contact. Animals have even been brought into nursing homes to provide more opportunities for warm, living touch. Yet we neglect the humans right under our noses who need every bit as much contact as an aging adult.

There is, however, one major difference between lack of touch in an older person and lack of physical contact with a child. Children, given their physical and social agility, can and will acquire touch whenever they consciously or subconsciously feel it is needed. But they won't necessarily get it how or where we would choose for them to do so! All human beings need physical contact in order to thrive. If we aren't willing to give it to our children, someone else probably will be.

I know, from my own unprofessional study based on raising my four sons, that there are certain times in a young male's life when he tends to draw away from physical touch. I noticed this tendency in each of my own sons as they approached the age of six or seven and then again when they were about to enter puberty. The natural tendency for a mom during such times is to oblige—to withdraw her touch, thinking that to force the issue might cause an even greater distancing. We reason that our sons are becoming men and need their independence. The fact is, for the most part, they are not really pulling away at all. Given all that is going on inside them, they are questioning whether they are still worthy of a hug, or a pat on the shoulder, or having their hair tousled, or their hand held around a table when we are about to say grace. By our own withdrawal, we send them the message that, perhaps, they are not.

I often noticed that when I pulled a stiffened son toward me to give his rigid shoulders a hug or his grimacing face a kiss, a tiny, almost imperceptible smile would sneak its way across his lips—sometimes disguised as a sneer. A soft, gentle stroking of the cheek or a squeeze of a hand can communicate far more than a thousand words of love. I know, because my children have since told me so.

Just a few months ago, a photograph in the local section of our newspaper caught my eye. It pictured an off-duty police officer, dressed in a suit coat and tie, accompanied by his young daughter. She, too, was all dressed up, in a frilly Sunday dress with ribbons tying back her long brown hair. Father and daughter sat facing each other on a blanket by a lake. It was obviously a warm, sunny day, and the caption informed us that they were on a "date." The little girl poured tea from a tiny teapot, while her father lovingly gazed at her. I couldn't help but think how valuable that child must have felt, enjoying the doting attention of her father!

Undivided attention is another aspect of love that is absolutely essential if we are going to keep our child's emotional tank full. Time spent chauffeuring our kids to soccer practices or drum lessons or ballet classes cannot substitute for focused attention. Fabulous birthday and Christmas presents don't even come close.

Focused attention takes time and sometimes requires extra effort. When we feel least like giving attention to our children is probably when they need it most. We must be willing to put down our projects and lay aside our agendas to let our children know that they are worthy of our time, our attention, our appreciation, our regard, and, most of all, our love. Because it is not how much we love our children that counts, it's how much they *feel* loved that really matters.

One of the biggest issues that children deal with today is the feeling of being "left out." This may take place at school or during after-school activities. The problem has surfaced many times recently during media interviews with children, especially during the current rise in school-related tragedies.

You and I both struggled with this very same issue. For generations, the problem has been synonymous with growing up. However, the difference between its effect on previous generations and its tie to the tragedies which are occurring today is that, in the past, regardless of how lonely we felt at school, we knew that we had a mother or a grandmother at home who cared. We knew that there was someone there who would give us milk and cookies or maybe an apple if she preferred health foods. Someone cared about how our day had gone. Someone was there who had time to touch us, to look at us, or to focus her attention on us when we needed it most. Friends are far too fickle to fill in for the unconditional love that only a mother or grandmother can provide.

Let me add just one more thing. We receive a huge benefit as mothers when we make sure our children receive enough eye contact, physical contact, and undivided

To keep a lamp burning we have to keep putting oil in it.

—Mother Teresa

attention to keep their emotional tanks full. A child with a full tank is far less likely to misbehave than a child whose tank is on "E." A child who knows he or she is loved does not need to seek attention or beg for affirmation in inappropriate ways.

God has given our children the opportunity to interact with many friends. However, He has given them only one mother! It is important that you and I fulfill the role designed for us by being both leaders and lovers. Our children can only comprehend our love when we spend the time and expend the effort to provide them with valuable eye contact, physical touch, and undivided attention. Only with these can their emotional tanks be kept full. And only when their tanks are full will they respect our leadership.

❀ Have I made the mistake of choosing to value friendship over leadership in my role as a parent?

❀ In what special way will I provide undivided attention for my child this week that will show him how much he is valued and loved?

A Mother's Prayer

*Lord, help me to understand the type of
leadership and the depth of love that You want me
to convey to my children. Help me to begin to
love them—not only with my heart but also with
my eyes and my hands and my time. Help me
not to allow my own inhibitions or upbringing to
interfere with the way You would want me to
love my children. Give me a sensitive heart, dear
God, one that knows when my children need an
extra measure of my time and attention.*

Chapter Five

We Can't Compete with "Everyone Else's Mom"–She Always Wins

The thing that impresses me the most about America is the way parents obey their children.

—King Edward VIII

Kids are clever. Very clever! Somehow, without our consent, they entered each of us in a popularity contest with every other mom in the world. Believe me, this is not a contest we would choose to enter voluntarily. I happen to know that, no matter how hard we try, there is a gal, simply referred to as "Everyone Else's Mom," who wins every time. There is no way on earth our kids will ever allow one of us to take home the prize.

Let me tell you a few of the facts about Everyone Else's
Mom that I've been able to garner from conversations with
my own kids. Everyone Else's Mom has no problem letting
her kids stay up past 11:00 P.M. on weeknights, and they can
go to bed as late as they want to on weekends. Apparently
her kids never get grouchy.

She doesn't care if her kids comb their hair or wear belts to
hold up their pants when they leave for school. Everyone Else's
Mom lets her kids roller blade or ride their scooters to the
Circle-K for snacks after school, even if there are no sidewalks
and all the crossing guards have already gone home.

Everyone Else's Mom buys her children all
the latest fashions, and she allows them to
wear their new clothes whenever they want. If her kids stain
a new shirt with spaghetti sauce or rip a new pair of shorts in
the backyard, she doesn't get upset. She is just happy to
replace them with something even nicer.

Everyone Else's Mom makes all the beds by herself, picks
up the dirty clothes, takes out the garbage, and feeds the
animals. She is willing to do all these chores so that her kids
can relax and watch TV after a long day at school. She feels
that it's important for her kids to talk on the phone to their
friends for hours, so they can develop adequate social and
communication skills. I don't think she ever cooks vegetables
or monitors what her children watch on TV. And I've been

told she doesn't care if her kids drink six cans of Coke a day.

I have yet to figure out where she lives. Sometimes my kids tell me she lives at Michael's house, or maybe Jason's, or David's for sure. But if I get around to calling their moms, I am informed that no such lady exists at that address. She quickly disappears, only to reappear at another friend's house—one I don't know quite so well. I guess she just kind of flits from house to house, lending a helping hand or sharing advice. What a woman! I wish she'd show up at my house once in a while just to help with the laundry. But until she does, I guess my kids will have to fold their own clothes.

Seriously, one of our first tasks in taking on Everyone Else's Mom is to check out the facts. When our children inform us that "all the other mothers are letting their kids go bowling right after school," it's worth a few phone calls to see which mothers, and which kids, are *really* involved. Often Mrs. Smith's foggy, "I'll think about it," uttered during an interrupted moment of bill paying, turns into a factual, "Well, Susie's mother is letting *her* go." This, in some twisted, cataclysmic way, results in all the other mothers caving in and allowing their fifth graders to head to the bowling alley unchaperoned, while Susie's mother obliviously finishes balancing her checkbook. Our kids' "take" on the truth is often far from reality. It is our job to maintain clarity, and one of the best ways is through communication with other parents.

If, upon investigation, we find that all the other moms are indeed allowing their children to participate in activities that we find questionable or unacceptable, then it's time for us to help our child find a new peer group. And, by the way, if no one else has given you permission to decide which peers your child may or may not hang around with, let me give it to you right now! I've heard many parents bemoan the fact their authority was completely undermined by the influence of their children's friends.

"Well, why don't you stop letting them hang around with those kids?" I ask.

"We can't determine who our kid chooses for friends," they whine.

Yes you can. And you must! Parents have been doing it for centuries. Young William Bradford wrote in a journal he began when he was about seventeen years old that many of the Separatists came to America because their children were losing their faith. They were being influenced by the "great licentiousness of youth" in Holland where they had settled to escape religious persecution in England. They felt the need to seek religious freedom in a land that would not corrupt their children, so they set sail across the Atlantic on a historic journey to America. They were willing to suffer great hardship in order to establish positive peer relationships for their children.[3]

We took one of our children out of public school and placed him in a private middle school in order to avoid a group of children he couldn't seem to help gravitating toward. He wasn't at all happy with our decision at first. But it wasn't long before one of the more influential members of his little band of former friends wound up in juvenile detention, taking several friends with him. Meanwhile, our son blossomed in his academic and sports activities in a much safer environment.

It is very important for us to look at the leaders in our children's circle of friends and ask ourselves some questions: Where are these leaders taking my child? Is this where I want my son or daughter to go? Does this direction fit with the goals I have established for my child?

We must not ever assume, for even one minute, that our child will be strong enough to stand up to his or her peer group if things get headed in the wrong direction. How can we expect them to when we can't?

Not long ago, I was driving home from visiting one of my older sons at college. I had about a four-hour trip ahead of me. It was a beautiful Sunday afternoon. The radio station was playing my favorite music from the 80s. The car was running smoothly. I had the cruise control set a couple of miles-per-hour over the limit. (Hey, they give you five extra before they ticket you, right?) But it didn't take me long to realize that just about every car on the highway was blowing me off the road. They were zooming by and staring at me like I was some doddering old fool.

When a line of about six cars led by a white Altima passed me and pulled back in my lane, I decided to join them. Soon, we were all cruising down the highway at about 80 MPH. I knew it was wrong, but everyone else was doing it, including three more cars that had hooked onto the "car conga line" behind me. It seemed like the logical, even obligatory, thing to do at that time, given those circumstances.

Sure enough, as we flew across the bridge over another highway, a patrol car sped up the ramp behind us, flew past nine of us, and nabbed the leader of the pack. Immediately the rest of us slowed down and drove the speed limit—for about five miles. Suddenly, a green Ford Explorer swerved out from the middle of the group and took the lead. Soon, all of us were once again traveling about 80 MPH. Wouldn't you know it. Another patrol car—this one was hiding in the trees in the median—zipped into action. Flashing his lights and whirring his siren, he took out our new leader.

At that point I decided to slow down for the duration of my journey. As I drove along all by myself, I was startled by the realization of what had taken place. I had succumbed to peer pressure from people I had never even met; people I couldn't even see through their tinted glass windows; people I had nothing more in common with than the desire to get somewhere quickly! My actions made me realize how terribly vulnerable our children are to the pressures they perceive from the "friends" who surround them. I set my cruise control at seventy, the actual speed limit, and settled in for a long ride home.

We all need authority figures in our lives to keep us within safe limits and from crashing through prudent boundaries. Otherwise, we would unwittingly destroy ourselves. That's why God created parents. It is our job to keep our children from unintentionally damaging themselves. I can guarantee that we won't be popular in our role. (I didn't particularly love the officer who pulled over the driver of the white Altima at the time.) But our purpose isn't to be popular. It's to love our kids enough to protect them and to be their parents.

Besides our need to research the facts our children feed us and monitor their friendships, we are sometimes called upon to check out their rooms. I have a friend who believes it is wrong to enter her son's bedroom without his permission. She insists that it is his own private and personal space and that it should not be violated under any circumstances, even by his parents. Her approach means that she has no control over the music he listens to or the television shows he watches, since he has a TV set on his dresser. She has no clue about many other important aspects of his life. I've tried to tell her what I think about this, but she won't listen. So, let me tell you.

I think that we, as parents, not only have the right to check our kids' private lives, sometimes we have an obligation to do so. That does not mean that I am an advocate of snooping through our children's drawers and dumping out their backpacks whenever they leave them on the dining-room floor. I don't like snoopy moms, and I feel that our children have the right to privacy as much as possible. However, if I feel that my child is facing some difficulty that he is unwilling or unable to communicate to me, then, if I love him, I will do whatever is necessary to figure out the source of the problem, so I can steer him toward a solution. If this means reading his journal or checking out the Web sites he has visited on his computer or reading the lyrics to the CDs on his nightstand, then that's what I must do.

We must know what our children are doing . . . who they are hanging around with . . . where they are going . . . what they are listening to or watching on TV . . . which video games they are playing . . . and how they are spending their time on the computer. I don't believe it is wise to allow children to have their own personal television sets or computers in their own private bedrooms for two reasons. First, this totally kills any free time they would otherwise spend with family members. And second, there is far more trash on the airwaves these days than we can imagine. There is no possible way to keep our children from being exposed to it if we cannot easily monitor their choices. As much as they might gripe and complain, our children need to know that we love them enough to set boundaries for their lives.

However, as much as we try to keep our children from hurtful friends and harmful situations, there will be times when they find themselves entangled in situations that are less than ideal. A dismal fact about our society is that just about every party a teenager attends these days will involve alcohol and/or drugs. Even more pathetic is the fact that many parents, though aware of the situation, do nothing to stop it. Some even encourage such behavior by providing both the motive—attributing it to a "rite of passage" into adulthood—and the means: unhindered access to illegal substances.

Sometimes we have to love our children enough to allow them to be unpopular. If popularity requires alcohol consumption or drug use or attending parties where either is accessible, then we must accept unpopularity with great joy and work with desperate enthusiasm to fill up any blank spaces it may carve in our children's lives.

No matter how thoroughly we may try to ingrain in our teenagers' skulls that they should not attend certain parties, like ones where there are no parents home or where alcohol if being served, they will sometimes find themselves in difficult situations. Knowing this, it is very helpful to provide them with appropriate escape techniques in advance. With a couple of our sons, we preplanned a telephone message. If they called home and said, "Hey, I just called to see how you're doin'," we knew it was time to show up and give them a ride home. We knew that the party had gotten out of hand. When we drove up to retrieve them, it appeared to be our fault that they had to leave, not theirs. Our children had our complete permission to use us as the "bad guys" whenever they needed to escape complicated peer positions.

We have come to a crisis point when many parents are questioning themselves and their ability to make a difference in their children's lives. And the rest of society is looking at parents in an accusatory fashion, wondering if they are doing enough to raise their kids.

—John Borkowski

We can and must make a difference in our children's lives. It doesn't matter what Everyone Else and Their Mothers are doing, we have a very important task to accomplish, and we are the ones in charge of the outcome. Everyone Else's Mom may allow her kids to participate in an activity, but it is our duty to check out all the facts before we allow our kids to take part. Everyone Else's Mom may allow her kids to hang out with the crowd, but it is our responsibility to investigate the leaders and determine where they are taking our children. Everyone Else's Mom might believe in total privacy for her children, but it is our obligation to step into their world when we feel there is a need. Yes, we are being judged, but it is not a popularity contest where our personal attractiveness is the deciding factor. It is more like an art show where the value of the finished project determines the prize. How our children turn out is *our* responsibility.

✿ Am I comfortable that my child's private life is healthy and happy?

✿ Does my child know how to count on me to bail him/her out of a difficult situation?

A Mother's Prayer

Lord, help me to be willing to stand up for what is right and best in my children's lives no matter how unpopular it may make me at the moment. Show me when they are in danger of being drawn into unsuitable activities or influenced by the wrong crowds. Make my decisions wise and my dictates clear. Give me a strong heart, dear God, one that is not afraid to do what's best for my children.

Chapter Six

For Every "No" There Should Be An Equally Attractive "Yes"

The word "no" carries a lot more meaning when spoken by a parent who also knows how to say "yes."

—Joyce Maynard

Mighty Moms have sticky floors and toothpaste on their countertops. Mighty Moms have to look past the fingerprints to see through the sliding glass door. Mighty Moms let their kids wear unmatched shoes to the grocery store. Mighty Moms don't get upset when they find the gravy ladle in the sandbox. Mighty Moms cry—but only for a few minutes—when their favorite T-shirt is acciden-tally stained with Kool-Aid or their antique picture frame goes crashing to the floor.

That's because Mighty Moms have learned what is really important in life. They are aware that a child blossoms in an atmosphere of acceptance and approval but withers when the climate is hot and heavy. They understand that too many rules and regulations can create an environ-ment of gloominess and frustration that will eventually lead to rebellion. They've learned that dwelling on the negatives depresses and damages relationships. Let me tell you how I first learned this lesson.

I was more than eight months pregnant with my first child and had run to the mall to pick up the last few things that I needed to complete the baby's layette. I was walking down the concourse when suddenly I felt a strange thumping sensation on the *outside* of my abdomen. It was quite different from the kicking and squirming that I had grown used to on the *inside* when the baby was trying to rearrange my ribcage. I knew something was up.

I glanced down and couldn't believe it. A little old lady was jabbing her gnarled index finger right into my stomach!

I jumped back. *How rude of her!* I thought. *How dare she touch me? This is my private space. It isn't my fault that I'm taking up a little more than usual.*

"Young lady," she said, not the least bit repelled by my angry scowl. "May I just give you one piece of advice about that wee one inside you?"

She didn't wait for my response but continued right on in her thin, crackly voice. "As you raise this child . . ." She jabbed me again just in case I wasn't sure which child she was referring to. " You need to remember one thing. Every time you give this child a no, be sure you give him a yes to take its place." She nodded emphatically, then turned and left. That was all she said before she hobbled away and disappeared into a bookstore.

For more than twenty years, I have been raising children. And for more than twenty years, I have never forgotten those startlingly delivered, yet very insightful words. Whenever one of my toddlers tried to grab a glass bowl from the dishwasher, I remembered that jab in the stomach and gave him a plastic bowl to play with instead. If an older sibling tried to swipe a baby brother's rattle, I remembered that crooked finger and taught him to make his own rattle using an empty milk jug filled with pennies. When our eight-year-old was invited to go on a last-minute camping trip with some classmates whose parents we had never met, he wound up having a blast camping out in our own backyard—thanks to the advice I was given by that matron at the mall. Replacing a negative with a positive became a way of life at our house.

As my mothering years progressed, I realized the invaluable wisdom of this impromptu lesson. I learned that raising children is a lot like growing a garden. We can pull the weeds all we want to, but until we plant some flowers or vegetables, our garden will remain nothing but a patch of dirt.

When we keep telling our children "no," and remove possibilities from their routines, we leave empty spaces behind. Our kids wind up with a lot of vacuous holes in their lives—holes that will eventually cause pain. They leave a crushing emptiness, a gnawing dissatisfaction, a dense feeling of worthlessness.

The only way to get rid of holes is to fill them up. And let me tell you something, if we don't find ways to fill the empty spaces in their lives, our kids sure will! Alcohol, drugs, sex—you name it—will fill in the loneliness and plug up the dissatisfaction just like putty fills a hole in the wall. They are not solid or permanent in any way, and they actually leave the structure more vulnerable than it was before. They just make things appear better for a while.

Before I go any further, I don't want you to misunderstand what I'm trying to say. There are plenty of very good reasons to say "no" to our children—but our "no's" must be very clear and very important. Our negative responses must be kept to a minimum, and any spaces they leave behind must be filled with positive alternatives. We must remember to keep our focus on what is really important in life—namely, the character qualities we have chosen to develop in our offspring. As they look back over their childhood, we want our children to remember the positive experiences they enjoyed with us much more than the negatives that we imposed on them.

To put it bluntly, we need to pick our "no's" carefully. (Forgive me. I couldn't help it!) Our "no's" must be

Each day of our lives we make deposits in the memory banks of our children.

—Charles R. Swindoll

important ones if we want them to really make a difference in our children's lives. And when a "no" is violated, it is our obligation to make sure that suitable punishment takes place. Consequences should be stipulated ahead of time whenever possible and must be followed through. Otherwise, we will totally undermine our own authority.

How many times have you stood in the grocery store checkout line behind a mom who threatens to smack the living daylights out of her child if he whines and reaches for one more candy bar? As the whining escalates into a full-fledged howl and the reaching turns into manic kicking and grabbing, the threats continue to upgrade. The child will probably wind up with the candy bar, the mom will no doubt go home with a headache, and meanwhile the threads of their mother/child relationship will continue to unravel and fray.

Two friends of mine were traveling with their daughters to the beach for the weekend. About half an hour out of town, one of the little girls started to complain. In a whiny voice she demanded, "Are we almost there yet?" The friend who was not the young lady's mother turned around and said, "Honey, that will cost you a dollar. We don't whine in this car. We will be there when we get there, and every time you ask about it, it will cost you another dollar." The little girl never whined again. And needless to say, it was one of the most pleasant trips her mother ever enjoyed.

If you stop and think about it, the violation of our "no's" can actually be an exciting experience. Disobedience elicits a concrete opportunity to provide a positive learning experience for our children. Our children should not only encounter firsthand the consequences of their violation, but we should use the incident to teach them correct behavior. Instead of just telling our children that something they did was wrong, we need to use the chance to teach them what would have been right.

When an older sibling snatched a toy away from a younger brother—which was a big no-no in our house since it revealed a selfish attitude—we would punish the offender by removing a toy from his inventory. The value of the toy and the length of the removal depended on the severity of the crime. Then we would take the opportunity to demonstrate for the snatcher how he could have obtained the targeted toy in a much more pleasant and easy fashion. We showed the offender how he could capture his baby brother's attention with another playable object, then easily slip the desired item out of his tiny grasp. It didn't take many repetitions to cure the disruptive behavior and restore peace to the household. Even to this day, our older sons are experts at making such subtle exchanges, and most of the time their younger brothers have no idea when they are being duped!

I can't emphasize strongly enough the power and the potential of positive parenting. For a child to thrive, there must be rewards for the good behavior as well as punishment for the bad. If we want examples of why and how we should use this technique, we needn't look any further than the Bible. We can use God as our example. Not a bad role model, I'd say. As He parented His children, the nation of Israel, not only did He describe for them the punishment they would receive if they disobeyed Him, but He constantly promised them wonderful rewards if they would obey His commands and do things His way. You could say He was luring them into obedience and good behavior. Call it bribery if you want, but I figure if it was good enough for God, it's good enough for us moms. And I've used this method for years.

Charts were a big part of our sons' training and growth. They were usually displayed on the refrigerator door, held there by magnets. They were bright and colorful, and they delineated the tasks that needed to be learned and any attitudes in need of change. Stickers tangibly recorded our children's progress, and drawings or pictures cut out of magazines registered the rewards they would receive when their obligations were met or their missions accomplished. The prizes weren't usually monetary or playable. They were things like bike rides together as a family or the privilege of choosing dessert at the grocery store. As our sons grew older, positive actions and attitudes were linked to special trips and car privileges—and, sometimes, frivolous stuff at the mall.

Positive parenting does not always have to involve tangible rewards. When our children do something right, we need to let them know. We need to find reasons to praise them as often as we can. This can be difficult for some moms, but it is a "have-to" if we want to maintain the love and respect of our children through their teenage years. I can't reiterate enough how imperative it is to be able to look into the eyes of each son and daughter, no matter what his or her age, and verbally convey to that child several reasons why we love him or her. We need to articulate our feelings when we appreciate something our child does. We must audibly admire some character quality that he or she is developing. Our child has to know that we are proud to be called his or her mom.

Yes, one of the keys to being an effective mom involves learning how to accentuate the positives and eliminate the negatives in our children's lives. The fewer negatives the better! They must only be employed when absolutely necessary, and they should be used to develop the character qualities we have already chosen to target. And they must also be consistently enforced. For every "no" we insist on, we must work hard to find a "yes" to fill its place. Empty holes in our children's lives can easily lead to wrong choices and unhealthy decisions. Positive parenting, including promises and praise, are necessary to maintain a healthy, happy, mother-child relationship.

❀ When my children are grown and look back at my mothering, will they remember me more for the positives or the negatives?

❀ How often do I praise my children? When was the last time I praised each child, and why?

❀ What kind of rewards do I give my children for positive behavior and character development?

A Mother's Prayer

*Lord, teach me to fill my children's lives with joy
and opportunity rather than vacate them with
negative decisions and decrees. Help me to ponder
carefully the importance of the rules and regulations
I impose. Give me the insight and patience to
discover "positives" whenever I am forced to deal
with "negatives" so that I don't cause their hearts to
become bitter or hard. Teach me to praise them
appropriately and to always fulfill my promises to
them. Give me a positive heart, dear God, one that
looks for the best in my children.*

Chapter Seven

Don't Underestimate the Power of a Bad Night's Sleep

Fatigue makes cowards of us all.

—Vince Lombardi

Much of the trauma that we face as moms is a result of exhaustion. And, to put it bluntly, most of the exhaustion is our own fault.

Think about it. When a child pitches a fit at the grocery store, it's often because he is too tired to behave himself properly. More than likely the trip to the store was just one more item on a long "to-do" list that we had to complete at the end of a long, draining day. The scene often scripts out something like this:

After retrieving Junior from preschool or the baby-
sitter's (arriving at least fifteen minutes late), we rush
to the video store to return an overdue movie. Then we

zip into the dry cleaners to pick up our laundry and stop off at the post office to mail a few letters. Finally, we head to the grocery store before we rush home to clean up the house and cook dinner.

So, after a full day at school or the baby-sitter's, our child finds himself being dragged in and out of his car seat, stuffed into an uncomfortable cart, then forced to keep his hands to himself while we whisk him down aisles loaded with stimulating goodies. His mind is begging for peace and his body is pleading for sleep. All the "goodness" he was allotted for the day has long since been used up, and sleep is the only thing that can replenish the supply. But instead of allowing him to take the nap he so desperately needs, we continue to overstimulate and overactivate him. And let's face it, by that point in the day we are usually exhausted ourselves.

So, we rush up and down each aisle, haphazardly tossing cans and cartons into our carts, praying that somehow we can combine them later to form some semblance of a meal. As we head to the deli counter, everything begins to unravel. Our child is too exhausted to behave, and we're too exhausted to do anything rational about it. Chaos erupts just as they call our number. (Don't tell me you've never felt like strangling a child when you were ordering sandwich meat at the deli.)

I'll never forget the time my two-year-old was swiping candy off the rack at the checkout counter while screaming at the top of his lungs and kicking his feet against the cart as hard as he could. I smacked his grubby, grabby little hands, held his flailing feet, and tried to stuff a juice cup in his bellowing mouth—all while I was attempting to write a check.

By the time the cashier handed me the sales receipt, I was distraught. My child was behaving so horribly that he had to be punished. I shoved my loaded cart back through the checkout line, wheeled it to the rear of the store, pulled my son from the seat (almost dismembering him in the process), and marched into the ladies' room. I had no clue what I was going to do, but somehow I had to calm him down and make him behave before we continued our afternoon odyssey.

As I passed by the bathroom mirror, I caught a glimpse of myself. The haggard face staring back shocked me. I realized how tired I was—and how tired I had allowed my son to become. Neither of us was fit to be out in public. I hugged my dear child, who immediately fell asleep on my shoulder, and I vowed never to be the cause of such chaos again, either in his life or my own. Both he and I needed more sleep!

Mother Goose understood the problem. Look what happened to Little Boy Blue. Can you imagine the trouble he got into when the neighbors discovered that his sheep had mowed down their meadow and his cows had chomped down all of their corn while he was catching up on some much needed sleep? I'm sure none of that destruction would have taken place if the boy's mother had insisted that he have a good night's sleep the night before. And what about that horrible little girl with the funky little curl right in the middle of her forehead? I bet she wouldn't have had nearly as many bad days if her mother had insisted she take a nap every afternoon.

God obviously understands the importance of a good night's sleep. Why else do you suppose He caused Adam to sleep so deeply before He introduced him to his brand-new wife? God knew that plenty of rest was a necessity if their marriage was to work, and He wanted Adam to start off fresh in the sleep department.

Seriously though, because lack of sleep limits our ability to think and act

> *I am convinced that a light supper, a good night's sleep, and a fine morning have sometimes made a hero of the same man, who, by an indigestion, a restless night, and rainy morning, would have proved a coward.*
>
> —Lord Chesterfield

rationally, it can have grave consequences in our lives as well as in the lives of our children. It produces many missed opportunities. It results in failed tests and triggers many devastating accidents. Accumulated lack of sleep can cause marriages to unravel, companies to falter, and churches to split. Sleep is food for the mind—it's what keeps it functioning. And we live in a sleep-starved world.

It is a fact that children who get enough sleep are less likely to be moody than those who don't. Studies show that the more sleep they get, the less behavioral and emotional problems kids exhibit. Rested children enjoy longer attention spans, have better recall, and are much more able to concentrate than children who are sleep-deprived. Children who get plenty of sleep recover from illnesses more quickly than children who don't. And did you know that growth spurts are accelerated with adequate sleep? That's because the human growth hormone is released by the pituitary gland during the deepest levels of sleep.

Knowing these things, it becomes our obligation as moms to insist that our children get enough sleep to allow their bodies to function optimally. Just because our child may not appear sleepy at bedtime does not mean he should be allowed to stay up. As a matter of fact, hyperactivity— translated: bouncing off the walls and ceiling—may actually be masking sleep deprivation rather than signaling an overabundance of energy.

As our children grow, we need to understand that their sleep needs and sleep patterns change. We all know that normal newborn babies need anywhere from 12 to 20 hours of sleep a day. They average about 16 hours, which, if we're fortunate, is divided into 3- or 4-hour naps between feedings. Toddlers and preschoolers need about 12 hours a day. Usually some of this is accumulated during an afternoon nap. Naps most often stop by the end of the third year, but this doesn't mean that a daily rest time should go by the wayside. Young children still need a quiet, wind-down period in the middle of their day—if for no other reason than their mothers desperately require it.

Bedtime rituals become important during toddlerhood. They help prepare a child to sleep by relieving anxiety and causing relaxation. Regular bedtimes and routines are far more important than we can ever imagine in creating a sense of security, love, and trust. Some of the best bonding moments I have spent with my sons came as I lay beside them on their beds, reading stories, singing songs, listening to their versions of the day's events, and praying with them. Bedtime often occupied close to two hours of my day as four different sons at four different ages with four different sets of needs were tucked into bed at four different times. But it is time I will never regret having spent.

School-aged children require less sleep, especially as they get older. Their sleep requirements drops to about 10 hours a day, although those with more intense activity levels will probably demand more. Bedtime rituals are still very important, despite the fact that the songs and stories often cease. I cannot emphasize enough the importance of hugging our children and telling them how much we love them as we put them to bed each evening, regardless of how old or resistant they become. The more a child seems to withdraw from contact, the more he or she *must* receive it! A good-night hug is a nonverbal way of blatantly stating, "I don't care how badly you were treated by your peers today, or how much you hate the way your body is growing, or how lost you feel in this great big world—I love you, and you are worth my time and my touch."

Teenagers require much more sleep than either they or we are willing to admit. Sadly and unwisely, we have allowed them to become the weariest subspecies on our planet. The average teenager gets about six or seven hours of sleep each night, yet their rapidly growing and chemically changing bodies require at least nine. Unfortunately the statistics surrounding their lives are showing the consequences of this deprivation. Teenage tiredness is associated with poor school performance, increased drug and alcohol use, and increased automobile accidents. It is even thought that this constant inadequate supply of sleep may play a role in the high rate of teenage suicides.

Homework, late-night rendezvous with friends, midnight chat sessions on the Internet—all of these things contribute to teenage exhaustion. And yet we permit them to continue. That's because we have allowed our children to manhandle our minds. They have sold us on the notion that *everyone* stays up after midnight, and *if we really love them* we will *trust them* to get enough sleep.

But I would like to challenge you with two facts: (1) Nowhere is it written that sleep deprivation is a rite of passage into adulthood. Rather, permitting it to occur is a form of abuse. To allow our teenagers to deprive their bodies of sleep is equivalent to allowing them to deprive themselves of adequate food or necessary medical care. Sleep is vital for their proper growth and well-being. (2) Nothing good can happen in a teenager's life after midnight. On the contrary, most of the trouble teenagers get into occurs after the midnight hour. Very few respectable places are open to solicit their business or provide entertainment at that time of night, and very few decent people are around to monitor their behavior. The only logical and love-motivated place they can be is at home and, preferably, in bed—regardless of what their friends are doing.

Sleep deprivation is the most common brain impairment.

—Dr. William C. Dement

Because most teenagers are not getting enough sleep on weeknights, they tend to play a "catch-up" game on weekends and holidays. However, researchers have found that this sends their circadian rhythms into a tailspin, resetting their biological clocks and leaving them with a constant feeling of jet lag. Instead of feeling rejuvenated, they often feel worse after their long hours spent "crashing" on the couch or "sacking out" in a dark bedroom.

Most teenagers don't see sleep deprivation as a big problem. It's not life threatening, right? Well, actually it can be. Drowsiness or fatigue causes 100,000 traffic accidents each year in the United States alone. More than 1,500 Americans die as a result of sleep-related accidents each year—and more than half of these involve drivers under the age of twenty-five. Insisting that our teenagers get to bed at a reasonable hour so that they can get a healthy amount of sleep may actually save their lives as well as the lives of others.

Because teenagers often stay up long after their parents are snoring, bedtime rituals seem to vanish completely. Yet, let me tell you what I have learned. If you really want to know what is going on in your teenager's life, the best time to find out is late at night. A teenager who knows that his mom will either wait up or wake up when he comes to bed at night is a teenager who knows he is loved. In our home, many insights have been gained, decisions reached, and feelings shared while eating late-night sandwiches at the kitchen table or while sitting on the edge of a bed or standing out on the front steps in the moonlight. Teenagers seem softer, more accessible, and more reasonable at night. Maybe their defenses are drained as the day wears on. Whatever the reason, it behooves us to be available whenever they are willing to be vulnerable.

If we really love our teenagers, we will insist that they receive an adequate amount of sleep. And we will attempt to entwine our lives with theirs in some meaningful way before they head to bed each evening.

Much of the trauma that confronts us as moms is due to lack of adequate sleep, both in our own lives and in the lives of our children. Many of the behavioral and emotional problems our children face are initiated or exacerbated by exhaustion. It is our responsibility to ensure that they receive the rest that their growing bodies require. If we love our children, we will insist that they go to bed at a reasonable hour—no matter how old they are. And we will initiate bedtime rituals that will cause them to know they are loved and secure.

❀ Are bedtimes in my family being set by me or by my children?

✿ What recent behavior problems or traumatic events in my family could be linked to lack of sleep?

✿ What bedtime rituals help my children feel loved and secure?

A Mother's Prayer

Lord, help me to love my children enough to insist that they receive the sleep they need in order to function optimally. Don't let me allow weariness to be a cause of any dysfunction or dejection in their lives. Help me to establish bedtime rules and rituals that are healthy and fun and that lead us to a closer relationship with each other and with You. And make me wise enough to get enough sleep myself. Give me a peaceful heart, dear God, one that is rested and ready for each new day.

Chapter Eight

White Can Wait!

Success is not the key to happiness. Happiness is the key to success. If you love what you are doing, you will be successful.

—Albert Schweitzer

As the mother of four constantly active, consistently noisy, completely male children, I often find myself longing for some of the finer, frilly things in life. Grungy baseball games have taken the place of graceful ballets. Plastic cups covered with athletic graffiti have replaced real glasses with etched designs. Indestructible wooden carvings have supplanted exquisite ceramic figurines. The only daintiness that remains in my life is in the form of three tiny crystal angels—and two of them have chipped wings.

But I think it's probably white that I miss the most in my life. White, as in freshly painted, unscuffed family-room walls. White, as in dainty lace doilies and crisp, cotton curtains that flutter in the breeze. White, as in magnolia blossoms picked early in the morning and set in a china bowl on the breakfast table.

Come to think of it, it was a *white* wedding dress that first got me into this mess!

Several years ago, while I was shopping for school clothes for my boys, I glanced over at the ladies' section and spied a pair of white shorts. They looked so fresh and cool. Sure enough, they were on sale. And, guess what—they were just my size. I *had* to have them!

That evening, just before we headed to the baseball field, I slipped them on. Suddenly, everything in my life took on a new feeling. The world became pure and soft and simple again. I felt brand new, refreshed, maybe even chic. I rejoiced in the memory and magic of white.

Of course I had to keep my six-year-old son at arm's length while he slurped his bright blue slush drink. My three-year-old wasn't allowed anywhere near me after crawling under the bleachers to retrieve a foul ball. The older two had to hold their own baseball bats and gloves as they balanced their sodas and pizza after the game. And I refused to put ketchup on my hot dog—just in case.

Wearing white turned out to be quite a pain. It was stressful for all of us, but I still felt it was worth it. *It looks and feels so good*, I thought to myself.

Then I got up to leave . . . only to find myself, and my new white shorts, inextricably attached to the bleachers by a gooey glob of pink bubble gum.

There are some things in life that just don't mesh with motherhood, and white seems to be one of them. For me to insist on attaching incompatible things to my life alongside my children is not fair. It dooms them to either frustration or failure—often both. One of my jobs as a mom is to ensure that my children are able to enjoy being children while they are under my care. In my life that means that white will have to wait!

Not long ago, one of my friends hired a decorator to help her redo her house. Together they found some antique mahogany furniture with curved wooden legs. They covered it in exquisite damask upholstery in gold tones. They chose the most expensive wooden blinds for the floor-length windows and painted the walls with delicately stenciled designs. I have to admit that her house looked beautiful.

The problem was, she had three little kids and a dog. The first week after redecorating, the dog chewed up one of the legs on the Queen Anne couch. The five-year-old snapped one of the slats on the wooden window treatment. And the youngest added some of his own doodles to the stenciled designs.

Simplicity and practicality are essential if we are going to raise happy, successful children. And we must to learn to prioritize. We need to ask ourselves questions like, "Is being able to wear a pair of white shorts to a ball game more valuable than being able to hold or help my child?"

"Is having a showcase home more important than providing a kid-friendly haven?"

"Does it really matter what the neighbors think about my lifestyle as long as I am doing what is best for my children?"

For several years we lived in the country. Our four sons played outside from sunup until sundown. One of their favorite pastimes was digging holes and burrowing tunnels. They spent hours every day planning and digging and playing down by the pond. But when we moved into town, I felt that huge holes in the backyard would probably not be an acceptable addition to the well-kept suburban lawns that our neighbors seemed to pride themselves in.

I was having a rather deep discussion concerning this matter with one of my sons when I was rudely interrupted by a shrill voice on the other side of our fence.

"Young lady! Young lady!" a wiry, elderly lady in a straw hat squawked at me as she arose from weeding in her impeccable flower garden. She gestured emphatically for me to approach.

Cautiously, I moved in her direction . . . stopping a few feet from the fence.

To laugh often and much; to win the respect of intelligent people and the affection of children; to earn the appreciation of honest critics and endure the betrayal of false friends; to appreciate beauty; to find the best in others; to leave the world a bit better, whether by a healthy child, a garden patch or a redeemed social condition; to know even one life has breathed easier because you have lived. This is to have succeeded.

—Ralph Waldo Emerson

"You listen to me now, young lady," my new neighbor addressed me sternly. "If that little boy wants to dig himself a hole, you let him do so. There is nothing more important for a young man of his age and stature than digging holes. It will show him what kind of person he is. It will teach him perseverance and patience and resourcefulness. It will make him feel successful. So you go about your important business, whatever that is. And let that little boy do his."

Needless to say, our backyard was soon littered with holes dug by happy, successful little boys—*very* successful judging from the look of our beleaguered landscape.

Not long ago, my husband and I filled in all the backyard holes and put down some sod. We decided that since the boys had outgrown hole digging, it was time to fix things up around the old homestead. We also promised ourselves that, by fall, we would save enough money to refurbish the dilapidated sectional and replace the broken coffee table in our family room. We were embarrassed when friends came over to watch Monday Night Football and had to hold their drinks in their hands and balance their chips and salsa on their laps for fear the table might collapse. We were self-conscious about the rips in the upholstery and the springs that occasionally chose to jab an unsuspecting . guest in the backside. We decided that, even though we might have to forego a few other pleasures, it was important to fix up the family room. So we started saving, and by the first of September the bank account held plenty of cash for a family-room makeover.

It was the Labor Day holiday weekend. For sixteen years our family had gathered at the beach to celebrate the end of the summer with one last fling before succumbing to the grueling grind of the school calendar. But this Labor Day we planned to head to the furniture stores instead.

Then, one of our rather disgruntled sons pointed out that with college coming up and ensuing careers, this might be the last year our whole family could converge at the beach to play in the sand and surf together. His brothers joined in. They insisted that new furniture was completely unimportant in their lives. Besides, they reasoned, it would cause a whole lot more trouble than the old. Their friends would no longer feel comfortable hanging out at our house. They wouldn't want to come over if they couldn't plop their feet up on something. And if we purchased a new couch or coffee table, such behavior would undoubtedly upset us.

Compared to family fun and unity, fancy furniture suddenly seemed inconsequential. We elected to spend our hard-earned money on a weekend rental on the East Coast. We realized that our four sons would rather remember boogie boarding on the breakers and wiffle ball games on the beaches than the comfort of a fine new sectional. We knew that they would prefer watching moonlight magic on the waves and sculpting huge sandcastles to placing their popcorn on a new coffee table.

You know, I could be seating my guests on a brand new settee and offering them hors d'oeuvres on a polished wooden coffee table right now, but I'm not. Nope. Instead I'm sitting on a tattered couch, holding a mug in my hands and remembering that weekend at the beach. I don't think our kids will ever forget scampering across the sand, chasing after scurrying crabs, or diving into the surf after wayward Frisbees. I hope they'll always recall the evening jaunts to the 7-Eleven for Slurpees and the annual trips to Inlet Charlie's to check out the 50-percent-off sale on swimsuits and surfboards.

The way I figure it, new couches quickly grow old, but family memories never become outdated. They never need to be replaced. They actually grow more precious with time. The ones we can't recall in our brains are neatly stored in our picture albums—which I'm going to set out on our new coffee table . . . as soon as we get one.

We must not allow trivial things—like white—to get in the way of producing happy, successful children. Too often we structure the contents of our lives so carelessly that our kids are doomed to fail rather than succeed. We must learn to prioritize, placing our children's success above our own pride. Simplicity, practicality, and kid-compatibility are vitally important components of a happy home.

❀ Are my children free to enjoy their childhood in our home and yard?

❀ In twenty years, what are some of the things that my children will remember first when they think of our home and lifestyle?

A Mother's Prayer

*Dear Lord, help me to program and prioritize the
things in my life in a way that will allow my
children to be successful. I don't want shallow,
trivial things to get in the way of their happiness
and contentment. Show me the freedom of
simplicity. Help me to understand the wisdom of
practicality. Give me a content heart, dear God,
one that is happy to adjust to the needs of the
wonderful children You are allowing me to raise.*

Chapter Nine

It's Okay to Accept Average—Excellence Is Highly Overrated

I suffer whenever I see that common sight of a parent or senior imposing his opinion and way of thinking and being on a young soul to which they are totally unfit. Cannot we let people be themselves and enjoy life in their own way?

—Ralph Waldo Emerson

"Eight-year-old William is training under one of the best karate instructors in the county," his mother proudly informed me while we waited to pick up our children from school. Karen was so excited and animated in sharing this news with me that I was afraid she might karate chop me into the wall surrounding the school. She related how, just a few weeks before, William had casually expressed an interest in the sport. She explained how she had used the Internet to investigate all the merits of incorporating such a program into his life. Then, of course, she proceeded to share each and every one of them with me. She described how she had spent several days checking out all the karate institutions within an hour-and-a-half of our town. She was sure she had found the very best karate school available, and she had enrolled her son. If William was to be involved, she was determined to provide him with ample opportunity to excel.

Unfortunately, all William wanted was ample opportunity to kick. A few weeks after paying his dues to the dojo in the neighboring town, William gave up karate forever. The fifty-minute commute twice a week, added to soccer practices and math tutoring and singing in a choir at church, plus the pressure of performing in a premier program, was evidently a little more than William could handle.

The push we put on our children to participate in numerous activities, and our preoccupation with excellence, is resulting in massive burnout in our preadolescents. And I believe that burnout is the number one, big-time problem in our preteens' and teenagers' lives. As more and more kids become engaged in larger and larger numbers of activities at younger and younger ages, it is my observation that fewer and fewer are staying involved once they reach their pubescent years. Therefore, at a time when our youth most need the camaraderie and consistency of organized participation, they find themselves sitting at home with nothing to motivate or encourage them. They've already tried and discarded just about everything valuable that society has to offer.

Burnout can trigger a rapid, downward spiral in our children's lives. First, it manifests itself as weariness or dissatisfaction. Then feelings of frustration and discontentment frequently prompt a child to drop out, which often results in laziness or feelings of uselessness—either of which can lead to depression. Depression can dead-end, quite literally, in the much more serious drug and crime related problems that face our teenagers today.

There are many ways that we, as parents, contribute to this epidemic of preadolescent burnout in our society. One is to involve our children in so many activities that they don't develop any enjoyable expertise or have enough time to experience any real pleasure in their activities. Children need some time on their own to work out any of the personal problems they experience with an activity. A child can't learn to dribble a ball down the soccer field effectively by spending two hours a week practicing with his team. He or she needs time alone to dribble around the backyard or kick the ball against a wall in order to develop the footwork that will give the young athlete confidence on the playing field. If life is a constant sequence of overlapping activities, no such time exists and no enjoyable expertise can be accomplished.

In addition to reaching an enjoyable level of expertise, much of the gratification gained from any activity includes the thought processes associated with it. Anticipation often provides half the enjoyment related to a particular pursuit, and evaluation provides much of the other half. The activity itself, although vital, is only a small part of the actual pleasure involved in the process. If children are rushed from one event to another and given no time for expectation or reflection, they miss out on most of the satisfaction and happiness they should receive.

Limiting the number of activities our children participate in is very important, but it is also extremely difficult. Our society inundates us with possibilities. Add peer persuasion and parent pressure to media overexposure, and soon we find ourselves carpooling kids to multiple events seven days a week.

One of the methods we used to avoid such overactivity burnout in our family was to limit each child to just two extracurricular activities during the fall semester of the school year and two during the spring. The choices were theirs. Any activity, within reason, was acceptable. But only two were allowed. One of the benefits of this system was the prioritization process our children had to learn. They didn't just sign up for any old activity helter-skelter. A lot of investigation and decision-making preceded their choices. This caused them to approach the activities they had selected with a genuine enthusiasm and appreciation. Limiting their activities also gave them the time and opportunity to be spectators and cheerleaders at some of the functions their siblings and friends chose to enjoy—a rare occurrence in our "me-first" or "me-only" society. They learned that they didn't always have to be the one performing on center stage.

Let me put it to you straight. It is never our kids' faults when their lives are overscheduled. Let me repeat that in case you didn't catch it. *It is never the fault of our children if their lives are overscheduled.* Scheduling is the responsibility of the parents and, like it or not, that responsibility usually winds up falling on the shoulders of the mom. We are so anxious for our children to take advantage of every opportunity available—and heaven forbid that someone else's kids might participate in more programs than ours do—that we rush them from one activity to another without analyzing the consequences.

Add to this the fact that we are seldom satisfied with an average performance, and suddenly we have placed our children under a huge amount of pressure. We buy our children the best, high-tech bats that money can buy to play Little League baseball. They must wear the perkiest tutus for ballet, have the finest teachers at the school, and drive the snazziest cars around. We push them to test out with the highest SAT scores that tutoring can produce, join the trendiest clubs that society offers, and flaunt the finest figure that diet and exercise programs can create—all so that they can be "the best" in every area of life. Excellence is so idolized in our society. But average is often so much happier. When we try to force excellence in areas that God designed for our children's enjoyment, we cause nothing but frustration in their lives.

Our plunge into this excellence trap can take place so innocently. We can be standing in the line at the grocery store when we overhear a discussion about a new tennis instructor at the city courts. The conversation might go something like this:

". . . and he's absolutely fabulous with the kids. I can practically guarantee you that after a year of instruction your kid will get into college on a tennis scholarship if he takes lessons from this man! Besides, *everyone* who is *anyone* has already signed *their* kids up. If I were you, I'd get myself down to the club right away before all the time slots are taken."

In less than half an hour we find ourselves at the tennis courts, signing Susie up for lessons whether she wants them or not.

This happened to me. It wasn't about tennis lessons, but it did take place at the grocery store. Two ladies were in line in front of me. One of them wouldn't stop talking about her son who was a junior in high school. On and on she went about all the clubs he belonged to, the sports he participated in, and the offices he held. "It's hectic," she admitted to her friend, "but it's necessary if he wants to get into a really good college. You've got to have lots of activities on your resume´ or they won't even consider you." As she emphasized the words "really good" and "lots," her friend nodded in agreement.

My oldest son was also a junior in high school at the time. I started to think about his resume´ and what he had accomplished that could possibly make him attractive to a bleary-eyed resume´ reader. There was not much besides baseball. "Able to do a perfect imitation of Rain Man" didn't seem like qualifying material. Neither did "can jump a knee board across a wake with the best of them."

There was no way my son was going to be able to compete with students like this lady's son who had already traveled the globe, played the French horn at state competitions, and been to Space Camp at least a half -a-dozen times. He needed something better, something more excellent, in his resume´ if he wanted to go to one of those "really good" schools. I decided I'd better get to work and help him out.

"Hey, Zach, have you ever considered running for some sort of class office?" I asked him when we were alone that evening.

He looked around the empty room to see whom I could possibly be talking to. He pointed at himself with a gesture of obvious disbelief.

"Me?" he garbled around the chips and salsa he was stuffing into his mouth. "Are you talking to me?"

"Yeah. You'd be good at it," I continued. "It would be a great experience for you."

He just stared silently at the label on the salsa jar, but I forged ahead with my plan for his life.

"I didn't mean president or anything like that. How about vice president? You're smart and popular and, besides, no one else is running this year."

His sideways glance told me to bug off, but based on the conversation I had overheard at the checkout counter, I felt the subject was worth at least a little more effort.

"You never know. You might really enjoy something like that if you would just give it a try."

"Uh-uh," he muttered emphatically, shaking his head. His mouth was too full of salsa and chips to utter anything more eloquent.

I was obviously losing ground, so I decided to come clean.

"Listen, if you want to get into a *really good* college, you ought to consider it. It would look great on your resume´ and frankly, you don't have very much to put on one right now. Student government holds a lot of prestige."

He stopped in the middle of dipping a chip and looked me straight in the eye.

"Mom," he said bluntly, "the answer is 'No.' I don't do student government. I do sports, and I get good grades. If that's not good enough to get me into a *really good* college, then I'll just go to a normal one. I happen to think that there are plenty of good colleges out there that would love to have someone like me."

It is the common error of builders and parents to follow some plan they think beautiful (and perhaps is so) without considering that nothing is beautiful that is misplaced.

—Mary Wortley Montagu (in a letter to her daughter dated 28 January 1753)

A glop of salsa landed on his shirtsleeve. He rolled his eyes and licked it off. That was the last time I mentioned college resume´s. I realized that "getting into a *really good* college" was not one of the important goals I had set for his life. Being comfortable with himself the way God made him was!

Some parents frustrate their children by overemphasizing excellence in one activity to the exclusion of all others. This can be just as harmful and debilitating as burying them under a pile of different activities

Our sons played outdoors from the time they could walk. When they were barely three years old, they could dribble a soccer ball from one goal to the other, shoot a pint-sized basketball through a low-hanging hoop, and hit a wiffle ball clear over the garage. They loved backyard games, and therefore, their large motor skills were well developed.

So, when our sons first entered the youth sports arenas of life, they were a coach's delight. I can't tell you how many phone calls we received begging us to allow them to participate on exclusive traveling squads, or AAU teams, or competitive squads for any and every sport. Yet, we always chose not to. At such a level, each sport seemed to emphasize its merits far above all others and require participation in its activities to the exclusion of all others. We felt that involvement at this intense level would not allow our children the freedom to make wise choices in life. They would be locked into one sports arena for most of their childhood. We also felt that the level of stress often involved was totally unnatural and unnecessary at such young ages.

For some parents it's through a particular youth sport; for others it's through grades at school or music lessons.

Whatever form it takes, more and more parents these days seem to be trying to create their own little super heroes. But look around, Mom. How many Tiger Woods do you see? How many geniuses have you heard of who graduate from college at age twelve? Such superstars are just not the norm. Let's face it. Most of our kids are going to be average at almost everything they do. That's what the word "average" is all about—it applies to *most* of us and our children. And if we don't learn to accept that, we are going to be frustrated and make our kids miserable.

Whenever my youngest child attended his older brothers' junior high school football games, he would seat himself near the band, preferably next to the saxophone section. He loved the music more than the games. So I strongly encouraged him to join his elementary school band as one of his activities for the semester. We borrowed a saxophone, and he began to practice. It wasn't long until the screeches and the squawks turned into haunting melodies. He obviously had a gift. The band instructor insisted that we pursue his music further. Immediately, I sought private lessons for him, contacting the best instructor at the college nearby. After just one introductory session, he agreed to teach Jonathan, saying that he was one of the most natural musicians he had ever taught.

For over a year we rushed him to lessons and rehearsals and performances. A whole new dimension was added to our previously sports-entrenched lives. However, it wasn't too long until Jonathan began to balk at practices and performances, and soon he informed us, "Music is supposed to be fun. I don't like all this hassle. I just want to enjoy it."

We had obviously mistaken excellence on his part for enjoyment. To push him any further would have killed all the delight he had in music. He didn't have to be performing to take pleasure in it. We backed off and ended up returning the sax. Now, years later, music is a huge, wonderful part of his life—on his own terms. He plays the guitar and sings in a band.

It's hard to sit back as a parent and accept average, especially when we have already conjured up a glimpse of what excellence could look like somewhere down the road. But accepting average is often necessary. This is particularly true when it comes to schoolwork and the dream we all have of our children attending a great college.

Not long ago, one of my sons had a writing assignment to complete. It was an important, end-of-the-year term paper, complete with title page and bibliography. Of course he waited until the last minute and rushed through it the weekend before the assignment was due. Sunday evening, after he finished his writing and headed to bed, I found the paper lying on the kitchen table and decided to read it.

I was surprised by how well written the paper was, but I noticed at the end that each of his bibliography entries was incorrectly listed. I knew that his teacher had explained this to him, and I knew that he had a sheet filled with examples that she had handed out. Yet, in his last-minute rush, he had neglected to follow her directions. I seriously thought about correcting them for him, since it was on the computer and a huge chunk of his grade was wrapped up in this assignment. I planned to inform him of the corrections before he headed to school. But I knew that it would be a much better learning experience for him if I allowed him to find out the tough way. The teacher's red marks on the paper would be a lot more effective teaching tool than my explanation of any corrections I had made while he was in bed. It was a hard decision for me—I knew it involved at least one whole letter grade—but I finally decided that learning was more important than getting an "A" grade.

When we focus on visible accomplishments and convey the impression to our children that what really matters to us is their getting good grades, we create all kinds of dilemmas for them. Eventually that mind-set leads to situations where our children feel compelled to cheat. I believe that this preoccupation with receiving excellent grades, rather than focusing on adequate learning, has led to the rampant cheating that takes place in our schools today. If we know that our child has allocated sufficient time and expended adequate effort on a school project or in preparing for an exam, we should be thoroughly pleased with a passing grade regardless of whether it's an "A" or a "C." And if they do not receive a passing grade under these circumstances, it is our duty to seek additional assistance for them. A letter grade is not always the prime indicator of the amount of learning that has taken place. And, after all, learning is the reason our children are in school. Not grades.

Before you conclude that I am on an "anti-excellence" campaign, let me quickly add that there is room, and lots of it, for excellence. If we want to encourage excellence in the lives of our children, let us do it in the areas of character and service and caring and responsibility. Let us teach them to be excellent in their moral character and in their reactions and interactions with other people. Let us teach them the importance of always being trustworthy and dependable. Let us teach them to responsibly use the gifts that God has given them to make a difference in the world—not just to embellish their own status or self-worth. Let's take the time to look back at the character goals we established for them and pursue growth and excellence in these things.

Let's face the facts honestly: burnout is a major problem affecting our youth, and we are major contributors! We need to love our children enough to control their schedules. We need to limit their involvement so that they won't have to face the consequences of burnout. Our children should be given enough time to develop an enjoyable expertise and experience the pleasure of the activities in which they are involved.

There is no real excellence in all of this world which can be separated from right living.

—David Starr Jordan

We must be careful not to overemphasize excellence, particularly excellence in one activity to the exclusion of all others. We need to learn to celebrate "normal" and applaud "average" a little more often. Once again, the key to survival in this area is to stick to the character goals that we have established for our children and to seek excellence in the areas of moral character, service, and responsibility—rather than in accomplishments.

❀ Do I focus more on character development or excellence in performance?

✿ How much time does my child spend with the family each week, enjoying meals together and attending activities of other family members?

✿ What steps will I take to insure that my child is not going to suffer burnout?

A Mother's Prayer

Dear Lord, help me to rejoice in my children just the way You made them—to celebrate the gifts and abilities You gave them without adding my own expectations and desires. Show me how to focus on character more than accomplishment. Teach me to foster in my children the desire to serve others more than the drive to be successful according to the world's standards. Give me a sensible heart, dear God, as I help them plan their schedules and approve their agendas.

Chapter Ten

Sometimes We've Got to Bore Our Kids to Life

.The life of the creative man is led, directed, and controlled by boredom.

— Saul Steinberg

"Mommy, there's nothing to do. I'm bored!"

No combination of words can cause a mother to cringe any faster than these. They sound worse to our ears than the screeching of fingernails on a chalkboard. They are whiny words that we try to escape at all costs. Sometimes, fear of these words often drives us to the carnival of activity we talked about in the last chapter, where children are rushed from one activity to another with no time for reflection or evaluation.

Certainly we don't want to allow time for boredom in their lives! We have been led to believe that boredom is

one of the causes of drug use and one of the factors that
eventually drives teens into gangs; therefore, we must avoid it
at all costs. Well, let me tell you this—boredom is not the
culprit. To say that it is, is equivalent to saying that water in a
swimming pool was the cause of a child's drowning when
actually, it was his lack of expertise in dealing with an aquatic
situation that allowed the drowning to take place. And just as
an untrained child flounders in water, a child who has never
been taught to face boring situations in their lives will
flounder when suddenly caught in the middle of them.

No matter how full their schedule or hectic their
days, inevitably, a time comes in every child's life
when they find themselves face to face with boredom
and no one is around to bail them out. If this takes place
for the first time in high school, or in college when they find
themselves parentless for the first time, it is likely that they
will turn to other controllers to fill the empty spaces. If they
haven't been taught to find enjoyment in boredom, the door
to depression and outside influences is quickly opened.

Just as we provide our children with swimming lessons to
insure their safety in the water, we also need to provide them
with "boredom lessons" for use later in life. Moms should
begin to pass responsibility for free time to their children at a
relatively young age. They should be exposed to lengthening
amounts of time that is theirs and theirs alone to fill—times

when no one else is around to provide and program activities for them.

Playpens equipped with a few colorful toys provide the perfect location for a child's first short lessons in boredom busting. A baby who is left in a safe, protected environment within earshot—and eyeshot, if possible—of Mom as she types a paper or prepares dinner or gives a sibling a bath, will soon find ways to entertain himself. And from this entertainment will grow curiosity, ingenuity, and the development of all kinds of inner resources.

Older children sometimes need a little help in deciding what to do with a large chunk of free time. There is no problem in having some suggestions ready and in providing some materials to help carry these out. But we must resist the temptation to jump in and coordinate a plan or help them complete a project. Scissors and paper and crayons and felt and glue can be placed on a table and left to the imagination. Shovels can be provided for the backyard or flashlights handed out at night. But a child's ingenuity should take over from there. Warning: ingenuity and messiness go hand in hand. Just accept it as inevitable, and help them clean up!

Continuing with the water analogy, swimming lessons not only provide a child with a certain safety factor for later encounters with pools and lakes, they provide a child with a wonderful venue for hours of carefree fun. Michael's story provides a great example of this.

When my children were little, we often went to a large neighborhood pool in the afternoons to swim. Michael, who lived just down the road from us, would play all morning at our house. Often he would eat lunch with us. Every day when we left for the pool, we would invite him to join us. But every day he declined our invitation.

One afternoon, as my children were engrossed in a huge game of Sharks and Minnows, I noticed Michael in the distance staring longingly in the direction of the pool. I made a point to talk to his mother later that day. I asked her if there was any reason why Michael could not join us. She hesitantly informed me that, even though Michael was older than my sons, he had never learned to swim. She was sure he felt embarrassed that he would have to stay in the shallow end while even my youngest child jumped from the diving board.

The next afternoon as we headed to the pool, I invited Michael again, but this time I explained that each of my sons had taken lessons and I would love to teach him to swim if he wanted to learn. About an hour later, he showed up at the pool in a swimsuit and slowly joined me in the water. I reminded my children that Michael had taught them many things in life, and I informed them that it was our turn to teach Michael something. It was our privilege to teach him to swim.

Together, as if it was the coolest thing in the world to do, my sons joined in the lessons and kept encouraging Michael through every step. It wasn't long until just about every kid in the pool was participating in the beginning exercises that Michael was going through with us.

Michael kept up with everyone, and soon he was in the deep end jumping off the board. A big, exciting world was opened up to Michael, and that summer he developed a new passion in life—he couldn't wait to go swimming every day! What had been one of his biggest pains became one of his greatest privileges.

Although it can be dangerous, water holds great capacity for joy. So does boredom. The same privileges and advantages that result from taking swimming lessons, hold true for the mastery of "boredom lessons."

Nancy Blakely, author of *The Mudpies Book of Boredom Busters,* believes that boredom is "a prescription for adventure." She writes, "Boredom is an invitation to our own party of events. Not an instructor's or a parent's . . . When we accept the invitation, something magical happens. Passions are born. Interests are developed. An inner fund of resources develops. The same resources we use for a meaningful life." She goes on to add, "Without this fund, boredom can push our children to self-destruction."[4]

Rich Robertson, a potter in Dubuque, Iowa, emphasizes the importance of boredom in art. "It is one of the biggest launchers of ideas," he says. "Our kids say, 'We're so bored,' and I say, 'Get with it!' It fuels creativity."[5]

Some of the greatest discoveries and inventions and literary works were birthed in boredom. What was Sir Isaac Newton doing when that apple conked him on the head and impressed on his brain the existence of gravity? He was daydreaming under an apple tree.

I don't think necessity is the mother of invention – Invention . . . arises directly from idleness.

—Agatha Christie

Where was John Bunyan when he wrote *Pilgrim's Progress?* He was sitting in a jail in Bedford, England, with nothing else to do.

And what sparked Jonathan Diaz to pick up a guitar and begin to play? It was boredom—complete boredom. "Who is Jonathan Diaz?" you ask. Well, he's my son and I happen to think he's a really great guitar player. You should hear him! It was the last week of summer vacation, and Jonathan was sitting at home alone. His three older brothers were out of town, and so, it seemed, were all his friends. He had already seen the reruns at least three times of every TV show he was allowed to watch. He had used up every penny of his vacation spending money. He no longer played the saxophone. And he was bored. Completely. Thoroughly. Bored. Much to his dismay, when he complained, I put him to work cleaning out the family-room closet. That's when he came across my husband's old Yamaha guitar. It was the only relic left of Ed's hippie days, and it hadn't been played in about twenty years.

Jonathan opened the old, ragged cardboard case, adjusted the red-flowered strap, and slung the instrument over his shoulder. He fingered the strings delicately, then carefully adjusting rusty knobs, he brought each string into musical alignment. Then he began to strum, and it wasn't more than about twenty minutes until he had mastered a few chords on his own. He spent hours and hours during the next few days playing that guitar and exploring its endless possibilities. He never did get any further along on cleaning out that closet.

By the time school started the next week, we had refurbished the guitar and Jonathan had learned to accompany himself in several songs. Now, playing his guitar is one of the greatest joys in Jonathan's life. I cannot recall him ever complaining of boredom since that discovery just a few years ago.

So, what should we do when our kids begin the dreaded "Mommy, I'm bored" mantra?

First, we must be sure that the television set is turned off. Television only inhibits creativity and enhances passivity.

Then we should reply with some brilliant statement like, "Oh, you're bored?" This validates their feelings and shows that we are actually listening.

And we must be prepared to add something like, "Well, I have a whole basket of clothes here that need to be put away. If you like we can do it together, or you can find something else you'd like to do for a half hour."

Just make sure they don't turn on the TV.

Then give them something to look forward to. " . . . And when the half hour is up, we can all go swimming." (Or, out for ice cream or something else that will bring them pleasure.) It's important that we reward their efforts to conquer boredom at first.

On hearing such a response, it's amazing how often a child will apply himself to finding something fascinating to fill the half-hour slot you just defined in his life.

The best way to conquer boredom isn't to avoid it or try to prevent it. It has to be plunged into. Sooner or later our children are going to have to swim through boredom on their own rather than be carried to the other side. It's best that they face that time while we are there to teach them some strokes that will keep them from drowning.

❂ Do my children have enough free time in their lives that will allow them to face boredom and discover life on their own?

❂ How do my children usually handle boredom?

❂ How am I going to handle the situation differently the next time a boredom crisis arises?

A Mother's Prayer

Lord, help me to comprehend the potential of boredom and the need for my children to face its challenge. With my assistance, may they develop life skills and resources that will allow them to find meaning in monotony and replace boredom with brightness. Give me the wisdom to know the best ways to spark their imaginations and develop their inner resources. Give me an instructive heart, dear God, one that enjoys training my children to develop independence and creativity.

Chapter Eleven

We Must Turn Our Homes into "Safe Houses"

*The best way to keep children at home is
to make the home atmosphere pleasant—
and let the air out of the tires.*

— Dorothy Parker

No one was practicing gymnastics when my children and I took a tour of the YMCA. There was just an instructor, a couple of my kids, and me in a room filled with huge gymnastics equipment and lots and lots of bouncy padding.

Wow! Up to that point in their lives, my children had never seen a balance beam or a pommel horse except on TV. They stood in wonderment at the size of the room and the apparatuses that filled it. As the instructor and I talked about the logistics of obtaining a "Y" family membership, the children wandered over and began to sheepishly play around the uneven parallel bars which had been lowered to a perfect "kid height."

"Go ahead," the instructor said. "Let's see what you can do."

"Oh, they've never taken gymnastics," I interjected. "They won't know what to do. Besides, they might get hurt."

"They can't," she informed me succinctly. "That's why we have all the padding—so kids can experiment and not get hurt. Plus, I'm here to show them what to do."

Gingerly, my boys began to try things out. One at a time they jumped up and swung from the lower bar. Soon they began to pull themselves up and maneuver their bodies over the bar. Sometimes they would slip and fall into the pit of soft foam cubes surrounding the equipment. They would lie there laughing and kicking for a few moments, then bounce back up and try again.

Before long they were standing on the lower bar, reaching for the high one, swinging, and gleefully flopping into the pit when their arms grew tired or they missed the bar on a flying leap. The safer they felt, the more they experimented. Soon their little bodies were flying off every piece of equipment in the room. Needless to say, I signed up our family for a "Y" membership that very day.

Our homes should be like that gymnastics room at the YMCA. They should provide safe environments where children are free to experiment and are unafraid to fall. In order to offer such security, our homes need to be places of acceptance, order, reasonable expectations, forgiveness, and unconditional love. These are five components of a healthy and "safe home."

First of all, there must be *acceptance* of the child. The world they face outside can be a pretty mean place at times. But our children need to know that all meanness and hostility ceases to exist once they step inside the doors of our home. They must know that emotionally, intellectually, socially, and physically they will be protected within the walls of our house.

 We talked often with our children about this particular "safety" issue when they were young. As a matter of fact, we pounded it into their skulls. We wanted them to know that no matter how bad things were at school, no matter how much they were teased or treated unfairly, they would be completely accepted and loved when they were with family members.

In order to accomplish this goal, I would not tolerate bickering or fighting. I did not allow derogatory or degrading words to be exchanged between siblings nor any form of fighting to take place. There were immediate consequences for violations—like thirty minutes of being Mom's slave in the backyard. That sometimes meant having to work side by side with their previous sparring partner. Always, before any punishment was complete, both the offender and the offendee had to come up with something nice to say about each other.

Now, I don't mean to mislead you—our home wasn't a quiet little wonderland! We had four sons, and there was always some sort of competitive action taking place. Believe me, my boys can turn anything into a competition. As a matter of fact, I'm sure that if two of my sons were stranded on a desert island and found one lone coconut lying on the shore, they would find at least a dozen ways to compete with it. There would be competitions to see who could throw it the farthest, or roll it toward a target the most accurately, or keep it under water the longest. Sometimes the competitive action around our house got a little rough. That's when I had to step in—just like a gymnastics instructor steps in as a spotter to provide safety when things get a little dangerous on the balance beam.

But as they were growing up, I wanted each one of my children to know, with complete certainty, that they would never get "beaten up" in any way when they were with family members. The family was to be their main source of support. And if a child was struggling with a particular issue outside the family, we made it clear that it was up to all of us to help him through the difficulty.

Today, as they approach adulthood, all four of my sons count each other as their very best friends. Sometimes it has taken more than a little effort, but over the years they have learned to celebrate each other's differences and appreciate and encourage the uniqueness that each of them brings to the family.

For children to feel safe, there must also be *order* in their lives. Now I'm all for spontaneity, but for the most part, children need established routines in their lives that they can count on. For instance, they need to know that when they get up in the morning, Mom (and Dad, too, if possible) will be there to see them off to school. They need to have certain times to do their homework. They need to know when we count on them to do their chores and what time we expect them to be in bed. Routines offer a sense of security and achievement.

Maintaining order necessitates that we establish boundaries. Just as a society cannot operate soundly without laws and limitations, nor a gymnastics facility run smoothly without rules and regulations, neither can a home function safely without its own policies and guidelines. We must establish clear, consistent, enforceable rules that serve to train and steer our children toward the goals that we have already defined for their lives. Our children should have a basic awareness of the reason for each rule and a specific understanding of the consequences that will be applied when any one of them is broken.

Notice that I keep referring to those goals we established in Chapter 3. If you haven't written yours out yet, this would be a great time to do so.

Let me caution you about rules. We must be careful not to set too many rules for two reasons. First, if we keep adding boundaries to their lives, soon there will be no room for our children to grow in any direction. Rather than feeling safe, our children will begin to feel imprisoned and will desire only to escape. Remember, for every "no," there must be an equally attractive "yes."

Second, if we have too many rules, we can't possibly police them all. Believe me, policing the rules is one of the toughest, yet one of the most important, roles of motherhood. I can tell you from experience that there undoubtedly will be times when you will look at your children in despair—because they have just broken the same rule for the twenty-eighth time; then, at your husband in disgust—because he has failed to help you enforce it the last twenty-seven times. You'll think to yourself, *Why didn't I just stay single?*

I thought my youngest child, Jonathan, would never learn to comply with a particular rule we were forced to make. The rule stated that it was a crime to mess with any project that siblings had undertaken with their Legos or building blocks. The penalty was removal from the construction site. After each of the first several violations, I pulled Jonathan away and sat him on my lap to watch his brothers play, carefully explaining that he was not allowed to topple their towers. That didn't work. As soon as I set him down, he obliterated the project completely.

I decided to try a new approach. I attempted to include him in the activity by teaching him to add his own blocks to the construction. But after adding two or three blocks, he would invariably kick the whole thing apart. That having failed, I took him to the far side of the room and tried to help him build his own skyscraper out of another set of blocks. But the second I let go of his hand, he ran across the room and knocked their blocks to kingdom come. I tried distracting him from the scene and engrossing him in a storybook or interesting him with a wind-up car—all to no avail. He always darted back to the main construction site and demolished it completely.

Finally, when I realized that his older brothers were about "to do unto him as he had done unto their blocks," I removed him completely from their presence and shut the door. He was not allowed to enter until they let him in. Needless to say, there were several very unhappy moments in Jonathan's life. But by enforcing the consequence of breaking the rule, I finally got the point across. The next time he was allowed back in, Jonathan played quietly and calmly beside his older brothers.

When children violate the rules, they need to know that the consequences will be enforced. And, here's an extremely important point: when bringing violations to their attention and enforcing the consequences, there is *never* any need to scream. Perhaps I should repeat that a little more adamantly, (but just as quietly!): *We should NEVER EVER scream at our kids!* Screaming only heightens the emotions of an already sensitive moment and lowers our credibility. If we ever find ourselves raising our voices, we should stop, take ten deep breaths—it takes at least that many to dissipate the scream—and start all over in a low, quiet tone. It's actually a whole lot easier for our children to understand what we are saying when the decibels coming from our mouths aren't causing the dishes to rattle and the cups to clang in the kitchen cupboards. It's a whole lot more effective too.

If we want our children to be happy, we must establish homes for them that provide safe, necessary boundaries. We must enforce the rules that protect those boundaries. When necessary we must calmly and quietly implement the consequences for violating the rules. We must also be honest enough to reevaluate the rules once in a while and be flexible enough to change them when it is best for the family. And here's another important point. When there are no violations, we must praise them for adhering to the rules! Yes, it is vital that we commend our children for their efforts to live peaceably within the legal limits of our home. There is nothing like praise to promote or prolong positive behavior.

Maintaining order in a home also means that there are *reasonable expectations* placed on each child. This not only helps them learn to carry their own weight and readies them for the day when they will be on their own, but it causes each child to feel that he or she is a valuable and contributing member of the family.

Correction does much, but encouragement does more.

— Goethe

Accomplishing this involves assigning tasks that are specifically defined. None of us functions well unless we know what is expected of us. Although a task or two may be somewhat challenging, they should not cause frustration. Our expectations, of course, will change as each child progresses through life. As I mentioned earlier, we used sticker charts to instruct and motivate our children when they were little. Starting at very young ages, they had duties that offered them opportunities to develop feelings of pride and significance.

Many mistakes will be made along the way. Rules will be broken. Expectations will not be reached. Goals will go unmet. Because of this, I believe that *forgiveness* becomes one of the most distinguishing characteristics of a safe, happy home. Part of the padding that allows our children to walk away, virtually unharmed, from a huge tumble is the knowledge that there is forgiveness available—that there will be another chance—and that we will be cheering just as loudly for them to make it the second or third time as we did the first.

I must be very careful to point out here that forgiveness does not negate consequences. That would be like saying a gymnast who totally misses the pommel horse on a vaulting attempt still deserves a perfect score of 10 for the effort as long as she gets back up. No. Although she might only receive a 4.6 on her first attempt, forgiveness means that the next time she makes an effort, the slate is clean. She is starting all over again with a fresh opportunity to receive a perfect 10 with no points deducted for the previous error.

One of the biggest mistakes that parents make in our society is that we try to justify the actions of our children under all circumstances. I ran into this when I taught in a high school. If I felt it was necessary to make a phone call regarding a child's behavior, which happened only under dire circumstances, I almost always encountered disbelief and denial on the part of the parent. It made it very difficult to help that child grow and mature in areas where I knew he or she needed help both at home and at school.

I have to admit that I was woefully guilty of this myself when our oldest was in kindergarten. One day, Zach's teacher took aside all the parents of her male children as we picked them up after school. Evidently something had been thrown in the classroom, and something valuable had been broken. At least two of the boys had been involved. The teacher wasn't sure which ones, but she wanted us to talk to our sons and find out what had happened. If we found out that our child had been involved, she wanted us to explain how wrong his behavior was and ask him to apologize.

I looked down at my son's cherubic face and replied, "Well, I'm sure Zach wasn't involved. He wouldn't do something like that. But I'll talk to him."

We got in the car, fastened our seatbelts, and took off down the road. Suddenly a little voice piped up from the backseat, "But I *did* do it, Mommy."

"What?" I turned around and faced him in disbelief.

"I'm one of the ones that threw the football, and it hit the teacher's desk and broke some of her stuff."

I wasn't sure what to do. I was silent until we reached the next stoplight. Then I turned the car around and said, "Zach, we're going to go back right now, and you're going to tell Mrs. Sebring exactly what happened, okay? Then I want you to tell her how sorry you are."

I pulled back into the school parking lot. We found Mrs. Sebring all alone in the classroom. I informed her that Zach had something to tell her. He repeated his short story word-for-word, adding, "I'm sorry!"

Then it was my turn to apologize, which I did profusely, for naively assuming that my child was incapable of causing such a problem. Together, Zach and I arranged to make restitution for the broken items. Never again did I so idealistically take for granted the innocence of one of my children. We must not always stand up blindly for our children, because sometimes our children are wrong. If that is the case, the most important thing we can do is to provide them with an opportunity to admit their guilt and seek forgiveness.

This story also brings up the point that we, too, must be willing to seek forgiveness when we err. Notice I didn't say, "if." I said, "when." We have to be able to admit our faults to our children and seek their forgiveness if we want our children to learn the importance of honesty and to experience the joy of forgiveness.

Last, and probably most importantly, a safe house is a house filled with *unconditional love*. Unconditional love is not some kind of outrageous love. It is simply love that does not grow weary. It is love that does not change, regardless of the circumstances it may encounter. It is love that does not have to be returned in order to survive.

To feel loved unconditionally, a child must know that he or she is wanted and liked. Yes, I believe that "like" is a necessary component of "love" in the same way that I believe commitment is. I also believe that both liking someone and committing oneself to that person are matters of the will. They both involve making a choice.

Do not think that love, in order to be genuine, has to be extraordinary. What we need is to love without getting tired.

—Mother Teresa

I guarantee that your child will go through stages when you will look at him and say to yourself, *There is absolutely nothing I can think of that I like right now about that child sprawled across my living room couch!* During those moments, you have to make an active decision. You must choose to like that child regardless of the circumstances.

Then, you must begin a training process to make yourself do so.

The most important step in the training process involves time. *The more you find yourself disliking your child, the more time and effort you need to expend on him or her.* I want to repeat that because it's very important. The more you find yourself disliking your child, the more time you need to spend with him or her. That is the only way that you will begin to see life from your child's perspective. Proximity is a prerequisite if you truly want to learn to like someone. By spending time in their world, you may even learn to appreciate their responses to life. You will definitely increase the opportunities available to mold and shape those responses. Unless you have tagged along, you have no way of knowing where your child is coming from.

And while you are spending time with your child, you must begin to search for reasons to admire him. This is the second step in the "How to Like Your Child" training process. You must start looking for good qualities that you can admire—like the fact that she still washes her hair at least once a week or the reality that he has only one tattoo. Go ahead and write them down. This makes the good characteristics so much more tangible and real. Then you must verbalize them. This is the most difficult step in the process, but it is vital. You must express the things you like about your child aloud and enough times that eventually you are converted and your child is convinced.

The bottom line is this: It is not how much we love our children that counts. It's how much they feel loved. In order to feel loved, they must know that we care about them more than any other time-consuming event or activity in our lives. They must understand that we value our relationship with them more than we value good grades, neat bedrooms, or an "appropriate" appearance. They must hear us say it.

Unconditional love does not mean that we will rescue our children from every unhappy situation. There are times that unhappiness is an appropriate response to a life situation. If their favorite toy breaks, or a pet dies, or if they are not picked for the traveling soccer team, sadness is appropriate and even healthy. They need to go through it. No, if we want our children to learn to be happy, we can't always rescue them from their unhappiness. But we do need to be there to love them through it.

Let's review. In order for our homes to be "safe houses," we must first of all provide our children with an atmosphere of acceptance and encouragement. They must know that inside their home, they will be emotionally, intellectually, socially, and physically safe. Safety involves order and the establishment of boundaries. We must enforce the rules that protect those boundaries; and when they are broken, we must calmly—and quietly—implement the consequences for violating them. And remember, it is just as important that we remember to praise our children when they adhere to the family rules and regulations.

By having reasonable expectations of tasks our children can and should perform, we give them a sense of value and we help to prepare them for the future. And we must not forget that forgiveness is the distinguishing characteristic of a safe, happy home. Forgiveness does not negate the consequences of failure, but it does give the child a clean slate for a fresh, new start. We must not always be quick to defend our children's actions. Sometimes they are going to be wrong, and we must allow them to suffer any reasonable consequences their failure may bring. We must provide an example by being willing to admit our own failures and faults and seek forgiveness when it is needed.

The most important component of a safe and happy home is unconditional love—love that does not grow weary or expect to be returned. If we love our children unconditionally, we will also like them. Liking them involves spending time with them and attempting to understand life from their point of view. To make a difference, we must verbalize that love.

✿ What have I done to encourage each of my children today?

✿ Is my home a forgiving home?

✿ What do I like about each of my children?

A Mother's Prayer

Lord, I really do love my children, and I want them to know and feel that love. Give me the wisdom and strength to make my home a safe place for my children; a place they can grow happily without the fear of ridicule, rejection, or failure. Help me to teach my children the freedom of forgiveness and to enfold them in the security of unconditional love. Give me a devoted heart, dear God, one that is not willing to settle for a home that is less than what is best for my children.

Chapter Twelve

Kids Don't Become Independent on Their Own

Mommy, come help me do this by myself!

—Benjamin Diaz (age 3)

The scene on the six o'clock news was heartbreaking. Half-naked children were digging through garbage dumps, scrounging for anything they could redeem to buy themselves a piece of bread. The newscaster commented about how independent these children were who lived on their own in the streets of that particular third-world city. But he was wrong. Dead wrong. And his own story proved him so. It was soon very apparent how truly *dependent* those children were. Their aloneness did not equate with independence.

A child who runs forlorn through the streets of some major city living on his own is *not* an independent child.

Neither is a child who lives in the suburbs and has everything that money can buy—but lacks the supervision of his parents. Nor is a child who is raised in a good family structure, does well in school, adjusts easily to various social conditions, and handles difficult situations by himself with aplomb.

You see, childhood and total independence are incompatible. They cannot exist simultaneously. Physically, mentally, and emotionally a child must be taken through an independence training process before he is able to adequately function on his own. A child must learn to stand before he can take his first teetering steps; to walk before he can run; to add before he can multiply; to be responsible to take out the trash before he can be trusted with the car keys. Often the kids we think of as the most independent—the ones who are thrust into the outside world at an early age—will grow to be some of the most dependent people in our society.

Until its roots are firmly established, a young seedling grows best under the protection of a forest canopy or sheltered on the side of a mountain. When this security is not available, as in the case when a landscaper plops one in the middle of a naked backyard, the sapling must be fastened to a stake to keep it from washing away in a rainstorm or toppling in a heavy breeze. Children must be protected or anchored in much the same way. If security is not provided, they will grasp onto something in order to survive. They are rather indiscriminate about whom they choose to lean on. Usually it is the person most readily available. Yet, the choice they make will affect the course of their lives.

A couple of years ago, a news report contained a profound statement made by a drug dealer in inner-city Boston. A new minister had just moved into the neighborhood. As the pusher was showing the preacher around, he made this telling remark: "I'm there when Johnny goes out for a loaf of bread for Mama. I'm there, you're not. I win, you lose. It's all about being there."[6]

The drug dealer was absolutely right. The people who influence a child most are the people who are there— the ones who are close at hand when the child is in need. God intended for parents to be the ones to provide the greatest security and the largest influence on the lives of their growing children. To accomplish this, parents must be present in the lives of their children. We need to be the ones who prop up our kids until they can make it on their own.

Somewhere in the latter half of the twentieth century, our culture adopted a myth and converted it into a principle of reality. Fallaciously we began to propagate the idea that quality time with our children is more important than the quantity of time we spend with them. We could not have been more wrong! My experience insists that quality times are almost always the product of quantities of time. The most important episodes of "independence training" come at the most unexpected times. Priceless moments of opportunity cannot be scheduled into certain days or sandwiched between specified hours.

I would never have known what was bugging my eighth grader, causing him to withdraw and appear depressed, if I had not positioned myself in his life at every available instant and every conceivable angle for the two weeks it took to decipher the cause of the problem. Some of my friends insisted that he was just in the middle of a teenage funk. "All kids go through this. He'll grow out of it." But I knew there was more to it than that. This behavior was not at all like my child.

One day I plopped myself in the chair next to him while he was doing his Spanish homework. "How are things going in Spanish class?" I queried.

"Fine," he replied pretty much as I expected.

I sat there quietly for a while then asked, "Who do you sit next to in class?" I was merely trying to catch a deeper glimpse into his everyday life.

He named some names and continued with his work. I know nothing about parsing Spanish verbs, so I was of absolutely no value in this homework arena. But as I sat there silently for about five minutes, things began to pour out of his soul. He suddenly stated that he actually didn't like where he sat in the class at all. When I asked, "Why?" he replied that the guys sitting near him were jerks. "As a matter of fact," he revealed, "I not only don't like where I sit and who I sit next to, I don't like anything at all about the stupid class!"

I discovered that my son had held this opinion since a class discussion had taken place a few weeks earlier. The topic had been movie ratings. I couldn't imagine why that was part of the curriculum in a public school Spanish class until I later discovered that the teacher was a political activist who was very vocal against all forms of censorship and wanted to indoctrinate her eighth graders with her imprudent ideas.

Evidently, during most of the discussion, all the students involved agreed with their teacher that movies should not carry ratings. "Kids should be allowed to see whatever they want to see," they insisted. "No one should be allowed to tell us what we can or cannot watch. That's an infringement on our Constitutional rights."

Not being a particularly vocal student, my son had not spoken up. But eventually the teacher called on him for his opinion. He quietly replied that he thought ratings were a good idea. When asked to expand on his answer, he explained that he liked to know what he might run into before he walked into a theater in case there was something he didn't want to see.

The teacher was surprised. "Why, what could a teenage boy possibly not want to see?" she challenged.

"Well . . . I don't particularly like to watch movies that are full of sex and nudity," he replied quietly.

There were a lot of hoots and hollers from the class. Unfortunately, the teacher kept pushing. "Why? Does seeing a naked woman embarrass you or something?"

"Well, it makes me feel kind of . . . well, kind of dirty," he responded hesitantly.

That did it! The class erupted in ridicule, making all sorts of unkind slurs aimed in the direction of his manhood. It didn't matter that he was the quarterback of the football team or one of the stars of the basketball squad—he became the object of mockery for two weeks. I'm sure only a couple of kids kept it up that long, but he had been humiliated. He felt like a big chunk of his world had fallen apart. Upholding the morals and values he had been raised with no longer seemed worth it. He certainly did not look forward to walking into that particular classroom anymore.

Only because I was present for a significant span of time in my son's life was he able to find the will and the way to share that event and his feelings with me. I was able to listen—the most important thing I could have done. Then, I arranged for him to spend time with a youth leader whom he admired. I clued him in ahead of time concerning the situation and he was able to affirm and applaud my son's character and his true manhood. Our eighth grader learned that his peers weren't always correct. He began to feel that it was brave and very manly of him to have stood up for his own beliefs. The whole experience became an important step toward greater independence in his life.

Being present in a child's life is one of the most crucial aspects of being a parent. And one of the most influential places we can position our presence is at the dinner table. Sophisticated, five-year studies of twelve- to seventeen-year-olds done by The National Center on Addiction and Substance Abuse at Columbia University concluded that parental influence is the most potent and underutilized tool we have to help our children journey through their teenage years. CASA's surveys found that the more often a family has dinner together, the less likely their teens are to smoke, drink, or use drugs. They found that children in families that have dinner together only once a week are more than twice as likely as those who dine together nightly to smoke, drink, and use illegal drugs. In fact, each night a family has dinner together reduces the risk of substance use by their children. They also found that a child who gets through age twenty-one without smoking, abusing alcohol, or using drugs is virtually certain never to do so.[7]

Being present in our children's lives takes many forms—from bedtime rituals, to cooking lessons, to camping out together in a pop-up tent in the backyard. It might involve sitting beside them, teaching them how to study. I totally disagree with the professionals who say we should not help our children with their homework. Do you think a geometry teacher has adequate time and opportunity to transfer the complete understanding of an intricate math formula to thirty-two sophomores? Can a first-grade teacher possibly teach each child at the same pace how to decipher diphthongs? If you want to spend a lot of good time with your children, working on homework at the kitchen table is a good place to do it. Mind you, I'm not advocating doing their homework for them. I'm stressing the value of just helping them in the learning and understanding process. And just being there!

You can make a difference in our society just by being present in the life a child, whether it is your child or someone else's. Just by being a friend, a mentor, a sounding board —just caring enough to show up and take an interest in their lives.

—Dan Case

Realistically we cannot always be present at every crossroads moment in our children's lives. Therefore, we must be willing to inject other healthy role models into their routines. A sports coach, a teacher, a neighbor, a relative, a church youth leader—these are all possibilities of persons who may have a fleeting but powerful impact on their lives. There are times, even when we can be present, that it is possible for other individuals to have a greater positive impact on our children than we would. I guarantee that our sons and daughters will not always view us as heroes, particularly as they move through their adolescent years. But it is part of our job to provide worthy candidates to fill in. They are necessary in the step-by-step process of separation that ultimately leads to independence. They can provide valuable advice to our children and present visible affirmation of our teachings.

Teenagers seem all too anxious to facilitate and speed up the separating process that is a necessary part of becoming independent. As they whip their independence scissors around, cutting ties with anything that has to do with childhood, they sometimes inadvertently sever all bonds with their parents. Although progressive separation from parents is a natural part of "independence training," a complete severance before a child leaves home for college or the workplace is not really what he or she needs or wants. It is our duty to resecure the essential bonds, perhaps allowing a little more slack each time.

We may need to be willing to drop our kids off a block from a friend's birthday party, allowing them to saunter up to the door and give the appearance that they are totally independent—that no parents exist to interfere with their lives. This is okay as long as we stay attuned to who is going to the party and what is going on. Our children need to know that we care enough—in spite of their verbal protests—to find these things out but that we also love them enough to let them "look good" in front of their friends.

In other words, although we must still be present in our children's lives, as they grow older we must be willing to allow some distance. We must back off slowly, gradually allowing them to make their own decisions yet remaining close enough to step in the second a harmful one is made.

Risk-taking is involved in just about every step of the "independence training" process our children grow through. As they begin to make independent choices, they need to be allowed to take risks to discover their personal strengths as well as their limitations. It is our job to encourage positive risk-taking that will expand their potential without placing them in jeopardy. Sports, performing arts, and outdoors or wilderness activities are excellent ways for children to constructively push their limits. Supervised involvement in a stretching experience is the best deterrent to dangerous risk-taking, which will undoubtedly occur if positive alternatives are not provided.

Our third child is a big risk-taker. We faced a constant challenge to get him through high school without allowing him to make some seriously unwise choices. So, when he announced that he and several of his friends were going sky diving one Saturday, we were actually relieved. This was a risk we could endorse. It was one that would expand his self-esteem and help him reach for new personal limits. So we responded enthusiastically—and then made a few behind-the scenes phone calls to make sure he jumped in tandem with a qualified instructor. He was surprised and delighted with our support, especially when he learned that many of the other parents had pulled the plug on the adventure. He understood that our approval was a reward for many other situations in which he had used restraint and not buckled to the pressure of his peers. The experience was a thrilling one—and he has never asked to go again!

You cannot teach a man anything; you can only help him discover it in himself.

—Galileo

As our children pass from one stage of independence to another, it is helpful and fun to offer rites of passage. These traditions identify the fact that they have crossed the threshold of one phase of life into the next. They are tangible markers that applaud our youngsters. They congratulate our children for having earned our respect and celebrate the fact that we know they are ready to handle new responsibilities.

My husband and I presented each of our children with a paddle on the day he turned thirteen. It was a handmade, wooden paddle decorated with his name and some identifying paraphernalia, like a tiny baseball bat or cleats, etched into it. It was a symbol that said, "You are now a young man, and we will no longer treat you as a child, including the way we discipline you." Although we had never used a paddle and only rarely spanked our children, it was a sign that hung in their bedrooms to signify that they had graduated from childhood and would be treated and respected as adults. With it came many opportunities and responsibilities. It represented a milestone in their lives—one they all looked forward to reaching.

Memories and traditions are of great value in supplying security and strength for a child as he journeys down the path toward independence. They help anchor a child through the storms of life.

Remember, it is our duty to train our children to become independent and productive citizens. In order to accomplish this, the most important thing we can do is to plan to be present for a large portion of their lives. As I've said, we must not fall prey to the notion that quality time is more important than large quantities of time, since the most priceless moments of opportunity cannot be planned into our schedule. But realistically we cannot always be present, nor will our children always listen to us when we are. For this reason we must supply healthy role models for them to turn to for advice and affirmation.

And don't forget, risk-taking is an important part of each step toward independence. We must provide positive risk-taking experiences that allow them to expand their potentials and understand their limitations. In addition, traditions and rites of passage provide tangible markers that our children have gained our trust and are worthy of new responsibilities. They are welcome milestones on the journey toward independence.

❁ Who can I turn to as a positive role model for my children when I need assistance?

❁ What traditions have I established, or do I need to establish, to help my children identify independence milestones in their lives?

A Mother's Prayer

Lord, this is an area in which I really need Your help. It is so hard for me to know when to hold on and when to let go. Help me to schedule my life in ways that allow me to spend plenty of time with my children. Give me the wisdom to know how to guide them safely toward productive independence. Show me how to use traditions as milestones, when to seek the assistance of others, and what risk-taking adventures I should allow. Give me a wise heart, dear God, one that looks to You for guidance as I steer my children toward independence.

Chapter Thirteen

Go Ahead and Dance on the Dining Room Table

A good laugh is sunshine in a house.

—William Makepeace Thackeray

It's a safe bet that if you have a child anywhere over the age of newborn, your home is not as neat and clean as you want it to be. Chaos and kids go hand in hand. This is a fact that is understood and accepted by almost everyone. Everyone except mothers, it seems. But the earlier we recognize and resign ourselves to this reality in the process of motherhood, the better. Otherwise we will drive ourselves crazy.

At some point we have to come to grips with the fact that it's a complete waste of our energy to get uptight when we find a half-eaten grilled cheese sandwich on the bathroom counter or a bottle of shampoo in the silverware drawer. Frumping and grumping around the house because the gravy ladle is in the cat litter or the car keys were thrown out with the empty boxes of Chinese food does absolutely no good. Trying to keep French fries off the back seat of the minivan and school papers off the floor only leads to frustration.

There are multitudes of messes associated with motherhood. We can choose to view them as either a part of the privilege or a cause of great pain. I vote that we opt for making life merry in the midst of the mayhem. Motherhood is a lot sweeter that way. And it's a whole lot more fun.

We need to learn to look on the bright side in each messy situation. Say, for instance, you can't find the TV remote. It's still a safe bet that you know where the vacuum cleaner is. Surely no one else in the family has touched it in at least three years! So, why not go ahead and vacuum the Cheerios off the family room rug while you wait for the remote to appear? Who knows, you may find it under the recliner as you trace and erase the Cheerio trail.

Beside the havoc it wreaks on housekeeping, another perturbing facet of motherhood is its affect on finances. Face it, from the second we ante up big bucks for the first box of disposable diapers until the last child graduates from college, we will not be able to meander into the mall for another manicure without feeling guilty. No matter how much we try to rationalize it, we will find it difficult to justify spending our hard-earned cash on such a personal luxury.

But it's futile to fret about our financial woes. Somehow we will manage to get the kids braces when they need them—even if we have to drive around in a beat-up, old, un-air-conditioned car while we make the payments. Trust me, some way we will find the money to purchase each of them new outfits for their senior proms, even if it means we have to wear slippers to church because we can't afford shoes for ourselves.

What's more, when we take on the responsibility for housing and caring for these squirrelly little creatures called children, not only do our houses and finances become muddled messes in the process. Before long our calendars start resembling Einstein's chalkboard when he was deciphering nuclear fusion. I'm amazed that no matter how carefully I try to monitor and evaluate the number of activities my children participate in, new ones somehow manage to wedge themselves into every corner of my daily planner.

Given just these three frustrating facts of motherhood—messy houses, muddled finances, and mixed-up schedules—it is obvious that one of the greatest assets a mother can develop is a wonderful sense of humor. Yet, how often do we hear the delightful music of laughter welling up from the hearts and spilling out the mouths of moms these days?

Not very often.

Why is that, I wonder? Why are we so uptight? Why do we take life so seriously? Have we forgotten how to be nutty and joyous and crazy and fun? How many times have your children heard you crack up with laughter or giggle with delight in the last few weeks? How many times have their fears disappeared because you were able to introduce a little humor into a tough situation?

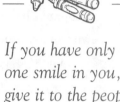

If you have only one smile in you, give it to the people you love. Don't be surly at home, then go out in the street and start grinning "Good morning" at total strangers.

—Maya Angelou

We need to take a good look at ourselves in the mirror. We need to see ourselves as our children do. We need to picture what kind of person they encounter in the kitchen first thing in the morning and envision who it is that greets them after school. Do they withdraw from the commander-in-chief of a homestead who rules with an iron fist? Do they quietly distance themselves from a whining, witchy lady who finds fault with most of the details of their lives? Or do they bubble with excitement, wondering what spark of joy Mom is going to add to their lives that day?

Not long ago I grew tired of the slovenly mess my youngest calls his room. I presumed that there still was a room under all the clutter even though I hadn't seen the floor in months. Years of begging, cajoling, and brow-beating him to straighten it up and put his clean laundry away had not succeeded in changing his habits one bit. His sloppiness had become a point of great contention—seldom with much comedy attached.

All else having failed, I decided one day to go the humor route. I bought a rat—a big, gray, plastic one that I happened to see at the department store. I placed it in the middle of the biggest pile of clothes under a shirt I knew he liked to wear. Sure enough, a few days later, as he was dressing for school, there was a startled yelp, then "What the heck is this doing in my clean laundry pile?"

It didn't take long for him to get the message and we all had a good laugh. And best of all, miracle of miracles, without me saying a word, he put his laundry away that day after school. Of course, the rat has come back to haunt me a few times—often lying in wait for me as I go up the stairs at night, but that's what makes life fun.

Not only is humor a great motivator, doctors define humor as, "a defense mechanism against stress." Dr. Judith Kupersmith, a psychiatrist at Texas Tech Medical Center in Lubbock says, "It's hard to smile and be sad at the same time." She points out that it is a medically proven fact that laughter can lower blood pressure. It releases little things called endorphins into the brain that make us feel good. Laughter improves our circulation, strengthens our immune systems and makes our hearts stronger.[8] All kinds of studies have been done in nursing homes and hospitals that confirm that humor enhances the quality—and often the quantity—of our days.

Cheerful people live longest here on earth, and afterward in our hearts.

—Anonymous

I know that I would not be able to survive a day of raising four rowdy sons, and living with their father, if it weren't for humor. It is the lubrication that keeps my life from creaking and groaning and eventually grinding to a halt. It's the vent that allows the steam to escape and keeps a situation from blowing up and causing great damage.

I can't forget a particularly dreary, rainy Saturday several years ago. The kids had not been able to go outside all day, and they were definitely starting to get on each other's nerves. I had sidetracked them, separated them, and even secluded them in attempts to maintain some modicum of peace and tranquillity. By the time dinner rolled around, everyone was in a lousy mood. The griping and complaining didn't stop when they came to the table. I turned the radio on and tuned it to an oldies station, trying to liven the mood a little, but even that didn't seem to help.

Nothing was suitable. None of the boys wanted to eat their broccoli. They insisted that they couldn't stand the taste of "little trees." They didn't like their meat 'cause they had hoped for fried chicken all day and now they were stuck with "yucky pork chops." The gravy had lumps, and there wasn't enough applesauce. "Besides, at Steven's house," they whined, "when he has to eat applesauce, his mother puts little, red-hot candies on top." But I didn't have any little, red-hot candies.

My husband started getting upset and demanded that they stop their griping. He said something sweet like, "Everyone shut up and eat everything on your plate, or there will be no dessert!"

Oops . . . There was no dessert. I hadn't had time to make anything, and I certainly hadn't wanted to run to the store in the pouring rain with all four boys. Now, everyone was really unhappy with me and my meal—including Dad!

Then one of the kids had the audacity to make a very disparaging comment about my cooking abilities. The gist of it had to do with the fact that if they had to go to school to learn to read and write, perhaps I should have to go to school to learn to cook. I don't recall who said it, but I do remember that things grew very tense as everyone waited for my response.

For the first few seconds, I was hurt. Then I was very, very ticked. I put down my fork and knife and pushed my seat back from table. Everyone was silent. I looked around at all the wide-eyed, little faces staring up at me, and suddenly the situation struck me as hilarious. I didn't like pork chops any more than they did. What a silly meal to have cooked on such a dismal day. Maybe I really did need to go to cooking school! I started to laugh.

"Well, you're right. I might not be able to cook, but I sure can dance," I exclaimed and started jiving to the rock-and-roll song that had just come on the radio. (I am a notoriously lousy dancer!) Soon little boys were twisting all over the kitchen floor and up on their chairs. I might have even hopped onto the table if we hadn't had a ceiling fan. Everyone cracked up and we boogied together until the song was over. I promised everyone ice cream at Davies' if they ate all their broccoli—and my husband promised to do the dishes if I stopped dancing. Somehow the complaints vanished, and we finished our meal. Every last morsel.

Joy is something we can learn. It is a decision we can make deep inside our souls—a decision to look at the positive side. The bright side. The crazy side of a situation rather than dwell on the darkness.

The laughter and the joy that flood our homes today will echo through them as long as we live. The fun and  delight we create will resonate forever in the memories of our children. We need to fill their hearts with happy recollections.

I remember my mother . . . she used to get to laughing some-times, so hard that she would get down on the floor and she would rock — all 180 pounds of her — and we'd be laughing with her. . . . Let's face it: each of us is a little cuckoo. Oh, the joy of getting in touch with that cuckooness again!

—Leo Buscaglia

We can't let our pride get in the way. I want my children to remember the fun times we had sleeping under tents made of sheets around the family room fireplace, even though every inch of the room was disheveled in the morning. I want them to recall all the times we played on the "Slip and Slide" in the backyard, even though it tore up the grass. I want them to laugh out loud when they remember safari hunts for stuffed animals on rainy days and clown shows on Mommy's and Daddy's waterbed. I want their voices to brim with enthusiasm when they reminisce about the long, adventuresome, cross-country trips we took in our big old van. I never want them to forget catching "crawdaddies" with Uncle Bill or spelunking through caverns with Aunt

Micki, or building dams, or watching tadpoles turn into frogs, or fishing with mussels they dug for themselves. And I want them to treasure our traditions—warming inside as they recall scavenger hunts for Easter baskets, backyard carnivals in the fall, and stuffing stockings for the homeless.

Some of our most treasured traditions began quite spontaneously or innocuously. Just before Christmas one year, our eldest son was bemoaning the fact that he had not been allowed to spend the night at a friend's house. It was a decision we made based on the fact that we had never met the parents. But "everybody else" was spending the night, and Zach was feeling very deprived. I realized that this was one of those "for every 'no' there should be an equally attractive 'yes' moment." However, Zach and his brothers were already in their pajamas, and we had just tucked them all into bed.

"I feel like we need to do something special for Zach's sake. He's really feeling left out," I pointed out to my husband. "And I think we need to do it tonight."

"Like what? They're already in bed," he replied, not really desiring to tack any more activities onto the end of his day.

"I know, but why don't we pile them all into the station wagon and drive them around, so they can see the Christmas lights?" I suggested.

He took a little convincing, but my husband finally agreed that it was a good idea. We marched into their rooms, flipped on the lights, and hollered, "It's time for a 'Light Ride' . . . everyone grab a jacket. You've got three minutes to get in the car!"

And off we went—all over town—looking at the wonderful light displays and singing Christmas carols. Going on a "Light Ride" became an annual tradition. Our children never knew which night to expect it, but always, just a few nights before Christmas, we would get them out of bed, bundle them into the car, and drive off to see the lights. It is a tradition none of us will ever forget.

The kids won't remember if the towels were folded and stacked perfectly in the closet. They'll remember if Mom was a fun person to be around.

—Kathy Peel

Fun times and memories should include both indoor and outdoor game times with our children. We mustn't stop playing with them no matter how old they, or we, get. Our kids need to know that we care enough to want to be a part of the entertaining times in their lives as well as the daily routines.

Whenever we go to the beach, our family has a huge wiffle ball tournament. Sometimes just our family is involved. Sometimes it seems that everyone on the beach joins in. I'm getting a little too old to go speeding around the bases, but if they need an extra player, you can bet I'm in, gimpy knee and all. If there are plenty of other players, then I'm the score keeper or the "ball getter"—a very vital role since the wind likes to catch the little plastic balls and see if it can transport them from the Florida beach to the Jersey shore.

Whatever my role, I want my children's memories to verify without a shadow of a doubt that I had a fun time raising them. When my kids come back from burying my tired, old bones, I want them to laugh not cry. While they sit around the church fellowship hall eating their ham sandwiches and toying with their potato salad—none of them has ever liked potato salad—I want them to recall with joy all the times I made them smile and all the traditions, games, and memories that we shared together.

✿ When was the last time I giggled or laughed out loud with my children?

✿ What fun traditions do we share as a family?

✿ What are some ways that I can add sunshine to my house today?

A Mother's Prayer

I admit, God, how easy it is to get caught up in the frustrations of motherhood. A messy house or muddled finances or a mixed-up schedule can quickly cause me to loose my joy. Help me to focus on the positive aspects of motherhood. Fill my house with sunshine. May it be a place my children remember with pleasure and delight. Let them recall my smiles and my laughter and the fun we shared together. Give me a humor- filled heart today, dear God, one that's not afraid to laugh out loud.

Chapter Fourteen

If the Grass Isn't Green Enough—Help Your Kids Spread Some Fertilizer

> Money is like manure. You have to
> spread it around or it smells.
>
> —J. Paul Getty

It was a late November afternoon. All four of my little boys were outside, taking turns playing with a radio-controlled car that they had been given several weeks earlier. The car was bright red with large yellow numbers. It could speed up and down the driveway, stop, turn on a dime, "pop a wheelie," and jump the curb. It was attached to a control panel by a long black cord. Each little boy would run at full speed beside the car when it was his turn to be the "driver."

For hours they played, as happily as could be—until George showed up, bringing along his huge, new, blue remote-controlled vehicle with spiky tires. It was bigger, brighter, faster, and could do many more tricks than the one my children shared. And best of all—it wasn't attached to the control panel by a wire. It just flew down the driveway all by itself while George sat on a stump, making it spin and spiral with a flick of his fingers or thumb.

Suddenly the little, red machine that had occupied so much happy time and attention was not good enough. My four sons each wanted his own Big Blue Bulldog with spiky tires and remote operation, just like George's. The whining and grumbling grew so great that I felt obligated to intervene. I sent George home and ordered all of my kids into the car. We headed across town— driving away from all the manicured suburban lawns, past the old high school, and beyond anything they recognized from our normal routine trips. Soon we were downtown, driving slowly by abandoned shops and rundown houses where the front steps were falling off the porches and trash filled the street gutters.

We spotted some children playing with a stick and some kind of homemade ball in a litter-strewn yard. I stopped, and I asked my sons how many of these kids they thought had a Big Blue Bulldog with spiky tires and remote operation. They looked at me like I was nuts.

"Do you think they might be happy if they had a little red car with a wire attached to it that could speed up and down the sidewalk, stop, turn on a dime, 'pop a wheelie,' and jump the curb?" I asked. "Or do you think they would pout and complain and act ungrateful?"

What a lot of things there are that man can do without!

—Socrates

My kids quickly got the point. Our little trip downtown helped to eradicate their feelings of being disadvantaged—at least for a while. Never again did they gripe about not having the latest remote-controlled vehicle. As a matter of fact, that Christmas they decided to give most of their toys away to less fortunate children. There was one family in particular, with four or five children all crammed into a small blue trailer, that one of my children wanted to "adopt." Matthew begged me over and over to take him back to deliver more toys—gifts he had just unwrapped.

Unfortunately children tend to have short memories. At least mine do! And experiences like these must be repeated many times in order to train our children in contentment. Contentment is definitely a learned habit. It doesn't come naturally. It has to be practiced and reviewed over and over. Trips to the Salvation Army headquarters to help with children's Christmas parties; serving meals to the homeless who frequent the Talbot House (a local soup kitchen); collecting books for an orphanage; providing baseball equipment for a needy friend. These are just a few of the events that I have used in a process designed to teach my children how fortunate they really are.

A discontented child is a child who feels incarcerated— hemmed in by his circumstances. Whether their confinement be physical, *"If only I was thinner or smarter or had smaller ears!"* . . . or social, *"How come I'm never invited to dances at the Country Club?"* . . . or financial, *"Why couldn't my father be a doctor, so I could have nice toys?"* . . . we must love our children enough to teach them that it is not the confines of the prison cell that determine the scope of one's freedom, it's the condition of the heart. They can be as free as they choose to be, regardless of the situation.

From inside a Roman jail cell, the apostle named Paul wrote to his friends in Philippi saying, *"I know what it is to be in need, and I know what it is to have plenty. I have learned the secret of being content in any and every situation, whether well fed or hungry, whether living in plenty or in want"* (Philippians 4:12).

Corrie ten Boom soared above the barbed wire barricades of a Nazi prison camp to share God's love with other women in the flea-infested barracks they called home, because she chose to see it as her own special mission field. Contentment is the ability to say, "This is what I have right now, and with this I choose to be satisfied!"

It is extremely difficult in our affluent society to get the concept across to our children that money, and the things it can buy, cannot create lasting happiness. It's hard to convince them that financial freedom has nothing to do with net worth but rather is found in a willingness to be generous with what we have.

Money never made a man happy yet, nor will it. The more a man has, the more he wants. Instead of filling a vacuum, it makes one.

—Benjamin Franklin

I'll never forget the Christmas my children begged for a trampoline. They didn't just beg—they pleaded and whined and cajoled. Somehow they convinced me that a trampoline would solve all our family problems. I think it was the line that went something like, "If you buy us a trampoline, we'll never, ever, ever ask for anything else for the rest of our lives," that finally converted me. So, I purchased a big blue trampoline and perched it in the backyard.

Of course, six weeks later they were begging for a puppy to play with on the trampoline.

The year your child receives his first boom box for his birthday, undoubtedly his best friend's little brother will be receive a stereo complete with surround sound for no apparent reason. At least that's what happened at our house.

When you provide your seventeen-year-old son with his first set of "wheels," a three-year-old Ford Probe, a neighbor will wake up just a few days later, on her sixteenth birthday, to find a brand-new Mercury Cougar parked in her driveway. This happened to us too. Well, I'm not positive it was a Cougar, but it was equally as good.

Undoubtedly at some point, your child will inform you that he might as well go live in an orphanage, where he can be treated like a decent human being. Yep. This happened several times as well!

These are the times when we need to, once again, wrench our children away from their grievances and drag them out of the house and deliver some food to a shut-in or take them to the pediatric unit at the hospital to visit a child with leukemia. Such experiences can afford them the opportunity to encounter a new kind of fulfillment based on inner character rather than outward appearance. It's the only way they will ever conquer discontentment.

If we want our children to learn true contentment, we must allow them to take significant responsibility for the things they desire in life. We need to let them demonstrate a desire to earn them and maintain them. For instance, if a child wants a puppy, he should help pay for it, care for it, buy its food, and take it to the vet. If he wants a car, he should help pay for the gas and be responsible for its upkeep. Or if a child wants to attend college, he must earn that right by applying himself to his studies and getting good grades while he's in high school.

I figure that it goes without saying that if *we* are not content with the lot God has given us as moms, our children will never be content with theirs. But just in case you're struggling a little with what God has provided in your life, let me ask a few questions:

1. What person, or persons, who made the headlines today would you *really* want to trade places with?

2. Compared to all the people who live on the earth today, how wealthy do you think you are? Remember, that includes all the zillions of people living in places like Calcutta and Sao Paulo.

3. Compared to all the people who have ever set foot on this planet, how fortunate are you? Think about the Great Depression and the time of the Bubonic Plague.

Do you get the point? Life is a whole lot more golden than we often view it when we forget to look outside our walls. When was the last time you reached outside of your family to help a needy person?

Yes, you and I have it pretty good. Our lives need to reflect a joy and contentment that is visible to our children. The way we react to our circumstances is the most important lesson that they can receive in the "contentment training process." We need to demonstrate satisfaction and display a sense of fulfillment in order to help them develop an understanding of what is truly important.

Not long ago, my aunt sent me a small sum of money and asked that I use it for something very special. After much thought, I decided to buy a once-in-a-lifetime birthday present for my husband—one that would benefit me as well. I planned a wonderful trip for the two of us to Cooperstown, New York. Now, that might not sound very exotic or romantic to you, but Ed has been a big baseball fan all his life and has always wanted to visit the Hall of Fame, and I am always game to leave Florida for a few days when the weather turns hot and muggy. I planned for us to stay in a little bed-and-breakfast inn where we could spend several, beautiful, cool days in upstate New York. I couldn't wait to go!

Plans were working out wonderfully, until we realized how much money it was going to cost us to send our son to the baseball academy we had promised he could attend following his high school graduation. The amount was staggering, yet, after much discussion we both felt that the investment in his life was important and, therefore, well worth the cash. It did mean, however, that we were not going to be able to take our trip.

The brochures are still on my desk, and the plans are still in my brain. Maybe one day we'll take that trip. But as our son has a chance to look back at the sacrifice we were willing to make for his sake and the contentment with which we approached it, we're sure that our small forfeiture will hold great significance in his life.

I believe that it is important for our children to understand the difficulties inherent in many of the freedoms they take for granted. It is our duty to help them comprehend some of the struggles that forged many of our national freedoms. They need to know what their own ancestors went through to allow them to be where they are today.

I don't think we should necessarily give them the old "walking barefoot in the snow uphill both ways" routine that my father liked to use. However, I think we should honestly let them in on some of the tough times we've weathered and the challenging situations we've endured personally in order for them to have what they enjoy. They also need to be allowed to share in the joy and pain of some of our current sacrifices, witnessing our satisfaction along the way.

Sharing and giving must be a part of our daily lives as we demonstrate contentment for our children. Back when history was first being recorded, giving was not only a way of life—it was the law. Levitical Law stated that farmers, which included almost everyone back then, were not allowed to reap to the very edges of their fields or gather the gleanings of their harvests. They were not to go over their vineyards a second time or pick up the grapes that had fallen off the vine. Why? They were instructed to "Leave them for the poor and the alien." (Leviticus 19:9-10.) They were not to cling onto everything that was rightfully theirs. Instead they were to share it. They were commanded to give away their extras— the things they didn't really need. For this, God promised to bless them.

> *Without a rich heart, wealth is an ugly beggar.*
>
> —Ralph Waldo Emerson

Wouldn't it be wonderful if we could weave this concept into the fabric of our family life? Most of us have far more than enough to live on, and it certainly wouldn't hurt us to give away some of the edges of our abundance. These edges don't always have to be monetary. We can and should give freely of our talents and abilities and time. We do this when we help a neighbor move, or mow a lawn without expecting compensation, or prepare a meal for a new mom.

A child who has successfully learned to be content, regardless of the circumstances, will be a relaxed child with an ability and freedom to enjoy the important things in life. That child will have a tremendous capacity to help others find pleasure as well.

❁ Are my children appreciative of the things that they have, or are they constantly wanting more?

❁ When was the last time my child had to take responsibility or work for something he or she wanted?

❁ Whom can we, as a family, reach out to and share the wealth that God has given us?

A Mother's Prayer

God, teach me to understand how truly wealthy I am. Help me to convey a sense of satisfaction and fulfillment to my children, and may we together experience the freedom that comes from being content. Help us to reach beyond our own lives to share with others what You have so generously shared with us. Give me a contented heart, dear God, one that is worthy of my children's imitation.

Chapter Fifteen

If We Love Our Kids, We Will at Least Try to Like Their Father

My mother buried three husbands . . .
and two of them were only napping.

—Rita Rudner

Think back to that beautiful day when you walked down the aisle dressed in a huge smile and lots of white lace. It could have been raining cats and dogs outside, but you were oblivious. You gazed at the man beside you with a deep, sincere love as your hearts and lives were joined together in holy matrimony.

Now take a few seconds to recall some of the most special romantic times you spent together in the weeks and months surrounding that event. More than likely, the thought crossed your mind on more that one occasion that, no matter what happened in life, you would always enjoy being with this man.

Admit it. Something at some point in your relationship attracted you to the man your children call "Daddy." If this were not true, those same kids wouldn't be running around the house calling you "Mommy." But I'm willing to bet that over the course of time, things have changed. Married life probably isn't as great as you once thought it was. And the man who fathered your children looks a little less like a knight in shining armor when not viewed through the candlelight of courtship.

Now, there are moments when you may find yourself feeling trapped and all alone in this project called parenting. You're not at all sure what your husband's role should be, but you're definitely sure he's not fulfilling it—at least not the way you want him to. You question whether the marriage will ever be a partnership again, and sometimes you wonder if it's worth sticking around to find out.

Well, let me tell you in no uncertain terms: it is! Unless there is physical abuse or severe emotional trauma involved, the best thing you can possibly do for your children is to learn to love, or at least respect, their father. Over the past several years, the many problems of children being raised in homes without fathers have been well documented. Besides the obvious economic repercussions, the absence of a father is strongly associated with psychological distress resulting in poor performance in the classroom, early sexual activity, teen pregnancies, drug abuse, youth suicide, and juvenile delinquency.

If you look at *any* measure of childhood well-being, you can see immediately that kids are placed at a much greater risk when they grow up without a father present in the home. What fathers provide is something unique and irreplaceable. The rough-and-tumble play they often engage in with growing sons can help those boys develop a healthy control over aggression. Daughters—especially those entering adolescence—benefit enormously from a close, loving relationship with their fathers. They do not have to seek self-esteem or search for their sexual identity in unacceptable ways if they know their fathers approves of who they are.

A mother and father actively parenting together is the strongest predictor of positive outcomes for children.

—Martha Farrell Erickson, Ph.D.

It is true that fathers parent differently than we do, but their part in the parenting process is vital and necessary. Even in those fatherless youth who seem to have escaped the serious consequences listed above, the longing for a missing father is profound.

For our children's sakes, we cannot afford to abandon or disparage the man they want and need so desperately in their lives. It will only serve to weaken and deteriorate our relationship with them. We must not ever lower ourselves to the point where we use our children as pawns in order to get even with their fathers, or view them as partners who substitute for the needs our spouses do not fulfill. Our children come equipped with radar that is highly attuned to tension and turmoil in our relationships. When it reaches an uncomfortable level, they tend to act out in an effort to divert our attention from the problems that could potentially turn their worlds upside down.

If we truly want our mothering mission and the whole parenting project we're involved in to be successful, we need to rediscover, respect, and communicate with the most important man in our children's lives. And we must commit ourselves permanently to the process. We need to start by reviewing the facts and rediscovering the feelings that led us into a lifetime commitment to him.

It was a spontaneous, almost pompous disregard for decorum that attracted me to the young man with the dark hair and broad shoulders in my chemistry lab at college. He began to show up at my dorm room at the most unlikely times to go for walks or to take me out for ice cream at a nearby stand. He would swoop me out of my study sessions to attend a concert or watch a basketball game. It didn't matter if we didn't have tickets or if the event was sold out. He'd find a way in. I loved it!

But eight years and two of our four children later, it drove me nuts! How dare he show up with an unannounced guest for dinner? Couldn't he at least call ahead to give me time to clear the laundry off the sofa, or clean the bathroom sink, or stick something other than pot pies in the oven?

And how could he expect me to pack up two kids and make arrangements to be out of town for a few days every time he had a last-second, weekend whim? Who would mow the grass, or be there when the plumber showed up, or call the soccer coach to explain why I couldn't provide drinks when it was my turn. No way we could just spontaneously jump up and leave. We had responsibilities in life, and he needed to get with the program.

Over time, I allowed what had been one of the most positive aspects of his personality—and our relationship—to become a nagging negative. What attracted me to him in the first place was about to drive me away. I had to get a grip.

I realized that it was not him or his actions that had changed. It was my perspective that was challenging our relationship—a perspective that had undergone renovation each time we had a child, every time we moved, and with any decision that required a new level of maturity.

I had to rediscover the reasons I had first fallen in love with and agreed to marry this man. Otherwise I was going to end up throwing the whole thing away—burying a relationship that was really only napping! But in this case, I was the one who needed to wake up.

I began to redesign my schedule, allowing extra time just in case unexpected activities leapt onto my calendar. I found a flexible baby-sitter who could help me out at the drop of a diaper. I discovered a few quick, new recipes and included extra food on my pantry shelves for unanticipated guests. I even tried to keep the hall bathroom neat and clean.

By anticipating the unexpected, there was room in my life for my husband's spontaneity. It began to be an attractive feature again. Once in a while I actually found myself hoping he would "surprise" me with a guest for dinner or tickets to a movie.

Yes, we need to look back at the man we married and remind ourselves what it was that attracted us to him in the first place. Then we need to find where those same qualities and traits are hiding themselves in the confines of our marriage.

And while we're at it, it might be a good idea to glance back and recall what it was that attracted him to us. It wouldn't do any harm to dress up for him once in a while like we used to. Sometimes he needs to know he's worth a little extra effort. Remember how much time it used to take you to get ready for a date? It's hard for your husband to think of you as the romantic young thing that swept him off his feet if the only accessory he ever sees you wearing is a dishtowel slung over your right shoulder or a scunci™ clip holding back your disheveled hair.

One of the biggest mistakes we can make is to try to manipulate change in our husbands. Often we feel it our duty to help them overcome their weaknesses. Let me clue you in on a little secret of marriage: it ain't gonna happen! I know you're nodding as you read this, because you've already tried it and failed miserably. God didn't give men wives in an attempt to make them holy. That is not why He established marriage. God's plan was for us to make our husbands happy. If they need to be changed, it's God's job to handle the renovations. He's much better in the holiness department than we are, and He won't get nearly as hassled in the process!

The only time a woman can really succeed in changing a man is when he is a baby.

— Natalie Wood

My husband used to watch football every Saturday afternoon while we were dating—and I was sitting right there beside him. So why did it surprise me so much when I found him glued to the television set every weekend once we were married? Sure, there were kids and animals and carpools and chores to take care of, but nagging him about them didn't do anything to change his passion or his posture. It just left me frustrated and hurt.

Before long I realized that altering such a core
characteristic of his male being would require something like
a hand-delivered message from an angel or possibly a well-
placed lightning bolt. And since I was incapable of producing
either, I decided that I might as well plan around his
Saturday ritual and take the kids to the park or the mall.
That way he was happy, and I was a lot less hassled.

We need to rediscover our mates personally, resurrecting
the viewpoints that once led to romance, and we need to
stop trying to revamp them. In addition, we need to learn to
respect the father of our children verbally.

One of the best ways to prompt our little ones to love
and respect us is for us to love and respect their dad. All men
like to feel esteemed. They want to know they are needed,
admired, and respected. Who doesn't? A key to happiness
and success in our marriages is choosing to view ourselves as
the principal prestige providers in our husbands' lives. We
need to practice praising the things our husbands do well,
while we quietly disregard the areas at which they are less
adept.

Not long ago, I noticed that our family room furniture
had definitely seen better days. The two-piece sectional and
matching recliner had been bounced on, sat in, and slept
upon by just about every teenager in town. They were
definitely wearing out. Then, during a male gathering to

watch a football game, the recliner completely broke. No longer could it be placed in an "upright and locked" position. Talk about "laid back." We continued to use it for a while, but it was very difficult to get in and out of the thing. Plus, the only way to view the television screen was over the tops of one's toes.

I turned it upside down and realized that one of the interior boards had snapped in two, so I decided to throw it out. I enlisted one of the kids to help me transport it to the curb for the garbage men to deal with.

When my husband arrived home, however, he had other thoughts. Realizing we didn't have enough money at the time to replace it and having recently viewed a fix-it show dealing with broken furniture, he felt inspired and obligated to fix it. Now, keep in mind that this is a man who has never fixed a faucet or salvaged a socket in his life!

So, the recliner was retrieved from the curb. Many trips to the hardware store, much sweat, and a little blood later, it finally sat fully upright in our family room. We were all very impressed as we gingerly got in and out of it and worked it up and down.

A short time later one of our sons, forgetting there might still be some fragility involved, plopped his big body in the recliner to watch his favorite show. In one "snap" three hours worth of work was destroyed. My husband was definitely dejected. A huge blow had been dealt to his male ego. He felt like a failure.

Before he could propel himself into a deep depression, I tried to console him. "Of all the people in the world who could fix this chair, how many of them would be able to stand up in front of a large, diverse audience and bring a book of the Bible to life, making it applicable to everyone in the room?" I wanted to know. "You are a wonderful teacher. In my opinion, that's much finer than being a fixer."

He didn't reply, but he did kind of smile.

Often there are times I wish he could fix things without messing them up. But that is just not part of his resume´. I need to rejoice in the wonderful qualities and characteristics he does possess. If I don't find reasons to praise my husband, you can bet that someone else can and will. And don't think he won't like it! Like a nectar-deprived bee placed on a columbine blossom, his heart will begin to buzz, and who knows where that buzzing will lead. There are lots of hives that would gladly house his honey.

Besides rediscovering him personally and respecting him verbally, it doesn't hurt us to show our love for our husbands creatively. Earlier we talked a lot about the necessity of communicating our love to our children. This is even more important with our spouses, and the same principles apply. Their need for eye contact, physical contact—aside from contact exclusively assigned to having sex—and undivided attention are no less than those of our children.

Love does not always have to be communicated in plain English. It can and must be conveyed in a variety of languages such as gifts, and meals, and candles, and back rubs. Little notes left under the pillow or written with soap on the mirror are inexpensive and exciting. A surprise date for coffee or an e-mail message sent to the office all help to demonstrate that we don't just take him for granted.

And if we're really serious about promoting prestige in our husbands and demonstrating our love, we will accept the things they love and respect. Often this means that we have to be willing to put up with some fairly unusual and, in our minds, largely unnecessary things that attract their attention—like sports talk and weird displays of power, including those that come from loud, roaring, machine-driven tools. There are very few men who don't pump their fists and growl through their teeth when they receive power tools for Christmas, no matter how unhandy they may be. My husband has a whole array of gadgets hanging on the garage wall. He is thrilled when he receives them and plans someday to take courses in how to use them.

Ed happens to particularly love tractors. This infatuation all started several years ago when we ran a camp deep in the piney woods of East Texas. The work was hard, the days were long, and the decisions my husband had to make were tough. One day, in an effort to get away from it all, he hopped aboard a tractor that had been abandoned near the barn, and he started to mow. He mowed, and he mowed, and he mowed some more—well into the starry Texas night.

From then on he has found it hard to pass up a tractor. Unfortunately there aren't many unkempt acres of overgrown weeds to be found in our suburban neighborhood, but there is always a baseball field somewhere nearby that needs a little special attention. After a long day at the office or a weekend filled with speaking engagements, my husband can often be seen high atop a big, green, John Deere-type tractor, skillfully maneuvering the base paths of a high school or Little League ball field. It makes him feel powerful. It pumps up his prestige. Gals, we've got to let them get their hands dirty and play with power tools if they want to—even if they're just revving them up.

Besides communicating our love and respect for our husbands, we must verbally communicate our priorities and desires as well. Believe me, our men will never figure out what we want if we don't tell them. I've come to believe that the burden of initiating verbal communication lies on the shoulders of the wives in most relationships. My husband can sit on the couch totally oblivious to the fact that I am huffing and puffing—desperately trying to vacuum the entire downstairs before out-of-town guests arrive. When I finally, in total exasperation, ask him to get off his duff and do something to help me, he responds quite nonchalantly with some ridiculous comeback like, "Why are you so upset? All you had to do was ask me nicely. I didn't know you needed help." And, believe it or not, he is telling the truth.

Before marriage, a man declares that he would lay down his life to serve you; after marriage, he won't even lay down his newspaper to talk to you.

—Helen Rowland

Often miscommunication occurs in our marriages because we just presume our husbands know what we have in mind or where our feelings originate. Or maybe we haven't taken the time to discover where theirs are coming from.

When my husband was asked to speak on a cruise ship headed for the Bahamas, he decided that we should take the children along. I thought it was a splendid idea except for one fact: they would miss a week of school. Having been raised in a very underprivileged home, then having worked my way through an Ivy League university, I felt that schooling was one of the most important priorities in my children's lives. To remove them for one week just to cruise the Caribbean seemed a bit irresponsible. It became a point of contention in our marriage. I felt we were headed in two different directions in raising the sons God had entrusted to us.

Finally, when we sat down to talk about it, I realized that we had exactly the same priority in mind. We both wanted the best possible educational experiences for our four sons. I just pictured them taking place in the classroom. He saw the teaching venue as much broader than that.

Once I realized that we had exactly the same goals in mind, I was able to accept his reasoning and make plans for a wonderful trip to the Bahamas. We had a fabulous, growing, and learning experience, not to mention fun. Consequently, it's amazing how many activities we added to our children's lives, relegating them under the category of "educational experiences." As a matter of fact, our family motto became, "Don't let school get in the way of their education."

Conveying, connecting, and coordinating our priorities are vital if a marriage is to work. It's pretty tough to go hand in hand through life when you're headed in opposite directions!

One last thing: I can't urge you strongly enough to *hang in there for the long haul*. We need unrelenting perseverance in this marriage thing if we want what is best for our children. Unfortunately, too many weddings come off without a real "hitch" these days.

Often there is nothing that lastingly binds the man and the woman who stood together at the altar. There is no lifetime commitment, no pressure for persistence. As a matter of fact, some vows actually state that they are in effect only as long as the two shall "love" rather than "live." Such a marriage is almost certainly doomed for divorce, because it can be guaranteed that almost every couple will eventually "fall out of love."

The first time I was made aware of this fact, I was shocked—and very relieved. I had begun to think my marriage was over. I no longer felt the spark that had first kindled our relationship. My husband no longer seemed to be the loving, caring individual I had married. As I have pointed out, even the traits that initially fascinated me no longer held much attraction. I was weary and ready to give up.

But two things caused me to hang in there. By looking around at my friends and neighbors, I began to recognize the effects that divorce had on the children involved. I saw kids struggling emotionally and socially, and I knew I didn't want that for my children. Then when someone pointed out to me that "falling out of love" with my husband was a common malady, I realized I wasn't alone—there must be hope. Women have been struggling with the same problem for years, yet over the centuries the majority of marriages have stayed intact.

Way back at the turn of the first century, Paul wrote a letter to Titus telling him to be sure that the older women—the ones who had *hung in there* for the better part of a lifetime—taught the younger ones how to love their husbands (Titus 2:3-5). Obviously, real love is a *learned* behavior. It doesn't just come naturally.

I found that the remedy for the "falling out of love" syndrome is bound up in one word: commitment. A commitment is very different from a contract where each side must hold up its end of the deal in order for it to stay in effect. A commitment requires only one signature. I found that as long as I opened myself up to the opportunity to abandon ship whenever I felt it might be necessary, I didn't feel obligated to do the bailing necessary to keep my marriage afloat. I had to faithfully commit—both to myself and to my husband—that I was in it for the long haul. Not liking things the way they were forced me to make some changes. I had to rediscover the man I married, develop a healthy respect for him, and learn to communicate my feelings and priorities. Actually, I'm still working on the last one. I'm a slow learner. I keep thinking he should know when it's his turn to change the cat litter without me having to tell him.

After reading this whole, long chapter, you may feel that none of it actually applies to your own situation. You may be facing the great challenge of being a single mom—either with or without your children's father in their lives. However, many of the things I've mentioned still apply. If you love your kids, you won't trash their father. As I pointed out before, if you want them to love and respect you, it is important to respect the man whose faults their unsullied eyes and hearts want to ignore. To the best of your ability, you need to build their understanding and estimation of the man they choose to unquestioningly adore—the father they long to know better. This means it is important to communicate with him and include him in their lives when necessary, even though it may be uncomfortable for you.

Whether we are still married to the father of our children or not, we must not allow past problems or personal pettiness to disconnect our children from a vital source of their being. We're big enough to overcome such problems. And God is a whole lot bigger than we are. He'll help us if we ask Him to. God wants nothing more than for our kids to grow up in ways that will glorify Him and make us smile!

✿ Do I view my marriage more as a contract or a commitment? In what ways can I improve my commitment?

❀ How can I show love and respect for my husband today?

❀ What special characteristic, talent, or ability can I tell my children about their father?

A Mother's Prayer

Lord, please help me to love my children enough to want to work on my marriage. Give me the desire to make it the priority it needs to be in order for our home to run smoothly and happily. I need You to rekindle in me a deep desire and love for my husband. Prompt me to respect and admire him. Teach me to communicate with him. Give me a committed heart, dear God, one that refuses to give up.

Chapter Sixteen

Bottom Line: We Can't Do This Alone

> Let your home be your parish,
> your little brood your congregation,
> your living room a sanctuary,
> and your knee a sacred altar.
>
> — Billy Graham

It was a balmy day in early June. The beautiful seaside town in New Jersey was just beginning to come to life for the summer. The lifeguards had recently resumed their seasonal duties, and the children, fresh out of school, were beginning to spend long, carefree days splashing in the surf and digging in the sand.

On that particular day, a twelve-year-old boy, having finished his morning chores, decided to spend his free time body surfing in the waves with two of his friends. Over and over they darted and dove their way through the surf to where the big breakers formed. And over and over they enjoyed the thrilling ride back to the shore.

Anxious for a little fun and adventure, the twelve-year-old boy's little sister had tagged along. She was not nearly as strong a swimmer as he and his buddies were, but she enthusiastically tried to keep up with their efforts in the tumbling and tossing waves.

The idyllic scene changed suddenly as the lifeguards, sensing a hidden danger, frantically began whistling for all the swimmers to come to shore. The three boys, realizing that the currents had rapidly and treacherously shifted, immediately swam to safety. It took every ounce of their strength and energy to make it in. The little girl, however, was caught in the undertow. Not strong enough to fight it, she was rapidly being swept out to sea.

The lifeguards whistled and wildly waved their arms—all to no avail. Even if she had heard them, the little girl was powerless to obey. Fighting for every breath of air, she desperately pushed herself off the bottom of the ocean floor only to have the current pull her back under and further out to sea. Over and over she fought her way to the surface for a gulp of air. Over and over she was pulled back down. Desperately she tried to save herself and swim to shore, but she was completely incapable.

By the time the lifeguards reached her, the little girl was panic-stricken. She grabbed and clawed at the two strong young men as they swam to rescue her, not realizing that her weak attempts only confused their efforts and made their task more difficult. Finally, her own strength vanquished, she suspended all effort and collapsed in their arms, allowing them to take control. Placing her on a rescue buoy, they fought the current and pulled her to shore. There was nothing the little girl could do to help. There was nothing she *needed* to do, except hang on and allow the lifeguards to do their job.

I know every vivid detail of this story, because I was that little girl—the first person rescued on the Jersey shore that summer in the 1960s. I clearly remember the feelings of desperation and terror that came when every ounce of effort I could muster was of absolutely no value. I experienced the futility of panic that can accompany the need for self-preservation. But I also recall the flooding, overwhelming sensation of peace that accompanied my complete surrender to a power much stronger than my own.

Most of us don't have the distinction of having survived such a harrowing physical ordeal in our lives. But many of us have experienced the very same feelings brought on by a compilation of emotional traumas—particularly when it comes to mothering. We've experienced firsthand the overwhelming feelings of inadequacy, frustration, and futility that have caused some mothers to abandon their roles and seek fulfillment apart from their families.

But do you know what? We have an even greater source of help and power available to us than those heroic lifeguards that saved my life on that disastrous day in June. Our help and power comes from God. And those of us who have allowed His strength to overshadow our inadequacies have experienced the sweet peace that comes with surrender.

For some reason, God, in all His sovereignty, chose you and me to become mothers. When He did, He knew very well that we were incapable of accomplishing the job on our own. He never intended for us to rely own our own strength and abilities. He designed the job to be a partnership—and He's the partner with the power.

> My help comes from the LORD, the Maker of heaven and earth.
> —Psalm 121:2

The problem is, we keep God in the background of our lives so much of the time that we seldom recognize His presence or recall His significance. Sure, we may try to fit Him into our schedules every once in a while. Some of us may even attend church services on a weekly basis. But when it comes to the daily routine matters of life, we totally neglect His presence and His power.

I know from personal experience that if we ever come to a place in our lives where we truly comprehend who God is—be it through teaching, triumph, or tragedy—and if we can ever begin to grasp what He is capable of achieving in and through and for us, we will no longer relegate Him to the back recesses of our lives. We will realize that He is far too awesome and too big to be crammed into some little cubbyhole of our existence. No, if we have ever experienced Him, we will never again try to fit Him into our lives. Instead we will beg Him to *fill* us.

The lifeguards on duty that June day in New Jersey didn't just happen to show up in the nick of time to avert the tragic drowning of a little girl. They were constantly on duty every day that summer, during the good times and the bad. Sometimes their job consisted of nothing more than giving advice to swimmers about suntan lotions or handing out Band-Aids for toes cut on seashells. Sometimes they posted water temperature readings or gave warnings of jellyfish in the shallow water. They cautioned children whose play became too rough and congratulated others who learned to swim. And, once in a while, they pulled frantic, little girls out of the swirling, gulping ocean depths.

That's how it is supposed to be with God. He is not on hand just to rescue us when we are in over our heads. He's there all the time—available to us for whatever help, advice, or companionship we need. But we have to be willing to take advantage of His presence.

Unfortunately we can often struggle with ego issues. Unless we are really messing things up, we tend to think too highly of ourselves and our own abilities. We may not see the need to seek anyone else's assistance—including God's. We rely on our own abilities as the key to success in the mothering process.

One day, my three-year-old and I had just left the house to run a few errands. On the way to the grocery store, we passed my mom, who lived close by. She was driving in the opposite direction and was obviously headed to our house. I had expected that she might arrive while we were gone, so I had left her a note explaining that we would be right back. Benjamin, however, was very upset when he saw her drive by.

"There goes Granny," he informed me excitedly. "I think she's going to our house." He banged on the window next to his car seat, trying to attract her attention. Realizing his efforts were futile, he became quite upset. "What will she do when she gets there?" he asked with obvious anxiety. "She won't know what to do, 'cause I'm not there to play with her!"

Granny, of course, was very amused when I relayed Ben's concern to her. It made us both smile to think that he felt that her happiness, and the brunt of maintaining their relationship, rested on his shoulders. Of course he knew he could count on her to help him out if things got tough, like when he couldn't reach one of his toys or had to tie his shoes or was hungry for lunch. But he obviously felt that it was his responsibility to take care of her whenever she was visiting or baby-sitting rather than vice versa.

Ben's warped perspective is amusing, but isn't that how we often find ourselves approaching motherhood? We feel that we are the most necessary participants. It seems apparent to us that it is our effort and resourcefulness that get the job done. Sure, God is there if we need Him to handle the really big things that we can't quite do for ourselves, but for the most part, it is up to us to raise our children. Right?

Fortunately this is not the same opinion God holds, nor is it the one He wants us to find ourselves burdened by. All of the wisdom, power, and creativity that we could possibly need for the task are available to us from Him if we will just avail ourselves to them. As a matter of fact, for us to try to make it through our mothering years without His help is ridiculous. It's every bit as futile and silly as trying to vacuum an entire house without ever connecting the cleaner to its power source.

I can't believe I'm admitting this to you, but I actually did this one day not long ago. Unbeknownst to me, the main hose on my Hoover had popped out of its clamp. I couldn't imagine why my efforts were so ineffective. No dirt or lint seemed to be disappearing from the carpet. Nonetheless, I kept right on vacuuming, going through all the effort and motion without any of the power! It wasn't until I had almost finished, and had become totally frustrated in the process, that I realized what the problem was. Although it appeared to be in place, the head of the cleaner was totally disconnected from the sucking source.

If we approach motherhood only on our own power, we might as well consider ourselves unplugged! We are totally disconnected from the awesome power source available to us. When we don't appropriate God's knowledge, strength, and creativity, we open ourselves up to all kinds of fears, frustrations, and futility. To place our children's lives totally under our own care is to limit the endless and ultimate possibilities that exist when God is in control. However, when we allow ourselves to be the "assistant" and allow God to be in control, all the pressure is off of us—and all His power goes to work.

To appropriate God's power, we must learn to pray. I can't claim to understand why or how it is that prayer works, but I know that it does. I know that prayer is the key God uses to unlock the vast storehouses of Heaven, and He has given it to us! It is an awesome treasure. If you aren't in the habit of using it, I would challenge you to start now by simply writing down your mothering concerns and turning them into prayer requests. You will be astonished as you watch God answer and work in your family's life.

For years I've kept a prayer diary. It's very simple and has just four columns. In the first column I put the date that I make an entry. The second column is for any needs, concerns, or requests that I want to pray about. I have labeled that column "I Ask." The third column is titled "God Answers." In it, I record God's resolutions to the requests I have made. And the fourth column is for the date that the resolution occurred. It is absolutely amazing to witness God's power and timing in my life. It is often so different than what I had planned or expected—but it is always perfect!

Over the years, I have kept separate prayer notebooks for each of my children and their own specific needs. Right now there is one beside my seventeen-year-old's bed. It contains some major requests concerning friends of his who are totally messing up their lives by making poor choices. There are personal requests like the one concerning finding new opportunities for his band to perform. A few requests might seem trifling or trivial to anyone else, like the one asking God to help clear up his skin. But all of them are important to Jonathan, and I don't think any of them are insignificant to God. As a matter of fact, I think they sometimes make Him giggle with joy that Jonathan cares enough to ask for His help.

The answers God provides are usually great cause for celebration and praise. It is an amazing exercise to look back over our prayer journals and see all the marvelous things God has provided and the powerful things He has done for us over the past several months or years. I find that it is much easier to look forward to the future with faith if I have spent time looking back at the past with thanksgiving.

Not only do we need to help our children record their requests, we need to spend time actually praying with them. They need to know how significant we believe God's role is in their lives and how important we feel their concerns are. And I would encourage you to share some of your own requests with them. It is important for our children to realize that we really aren't superhero "Mighty Moms," but that we struggle too. However, God gives us the ability to keep on going and the strength to handle tough situations.

Any attempt I make to describe the impact a mother's prayer life can have on her children would be inadequate . . . but let me try. When I headed off to college during the Vietnam War years, I had come to a place in my life where I truly felt that I did not need nor desire any kind of relationship with God. The more time I spent at college, the more I began to doubt His very existence. All of my professors seemed determined to eradicate any floundering freshman's faith.

On top of that, my roommate was a true "flower child," who espoused total freedom in love, speech, drugs, and whatever happened to appeal to her at the moment. At times, her lifestyle appeared very attractive to me. She was extremely popular and apparently very happy. But every time I found myself beginning to subscribe to her point of view and desiring to join in her extracurricular activities, a vivid image flashed through my mind. It was a picture of my mom on her knees beside her bed praying for me—a place and a posture I had witnessed many times.

I began to despise that picture, because I couldn't erase it or avoid its influence. And although it resulted in many lonely evenings spent in a dorm room by myself, that indelible image etched on my mind during my childhood years would not allow me to join my roommate. It wasn't just the fact that my mom prayed for me, it was the fact that I knew she was praying for me that possibly saved my life and definitely kept me from making many major sinful mistakes in those tumultuous college years.

It is not only important for us to spend time in prayer with and for our children, it is also important for us to understand the directives God has given us in His Word.

We need to spend time reading our Bibles, understanding its principles, and applying them to our lives. And we must create a desire in our children to do so as well.

We teach our children how to tie their shoes and ride their two-wheeled bicycles. We encourage them to develop friendships, and we help them resolve rivalries. We coach them until they can read and count and spell their names. We carefully guide them in many areas of their physical, emotional, and mental growth, yet we woefully neglect the most important aspect of their training and maturation— their spiritual development. At best we usually relegate the task to Sunday-school teachers who are allotted a one-hour slot each week to teach them everything there is to know about God and His perspective on life.

Often, instead of encouraging our children's questions and seeking answers, we remain aloof or unapproachable, promoting ignorance in the area of their spiritual growth. Instead of incorporating God into their everyday lives, we remain silent, making Him appear distant and uncaring. Instead of verbally passing on our morals and values, we hope that somehow they will "catch" them by just hanging around us. But believe me, it won't happen.

Children raised without a concrete understanding of God are lost. They go through life floundering—searching for meaning and identity. They have no security in knowing who made them, why they are here, or how they fit into the grand drama of life. Many of us have experienced this firsthand, as the philosophy of "permissive parenting" came into vogue during the latter half of the twentieth century. One of the tenets of this freedom-emphasizing parenting style is the idea that morals and ethics should not be taught until children are old enough to select their own value systems. Consequently, our families are now breaking all records for drug abuse, family instability, depression, and suicide as we search for meaning in life.

I can think of no greater satisfaction than the comprehension that the Creator of the Universe knows *me* and has a plan for *my* life. We need to introduce our children to Him personally. We need to teach morals and values and ethics if we want them to experience individual and collective peace and happiness. And our best teaching guide is the Bible.

It is our duty to make their spiritual training fun. Bible stories don't have to be read or told. They can be shared creatively, by acting them out, watching a videotape, or listening to kids' audio tapes. If you haven't checked out the inspirational section of your local bookstore lately, you will be amazed at the variety and volume of materials available to help make Bible study enjoyable for families. Teenagers can be led through theological discussions based on the lyrics of their favorite songs or the premise of a popular movie. We must never be accused of boring our children with the things of God. Our lives should be examples of enthusiasm and involvement when it comes to teaching spiritual issues.

And remember, if we want something to be learned by our children, *we* must not only verbalize it—we must live it out before them. If we want our children to be honest, *we* must be honest at all times and in all places. That means never fudging the facts on their absentee notes when they've missed a day of school. If we want our children to be content, we must choose to be satisfied with what we already have and not constantly desiring more. If we want our children to learn patience, *we* must be patient in the long checkout lanes and the crowded restaurants of life.

Any lesson offered a child in an abstract manner that isn't backed up by deeds is not going to work very well.

—Dr. Robert Coles

One of the best ways to reinforce the morals and values we choose to teach our children is by adding symbols to our verbal and nonverbal lessons and by building traditions into their lives. Somehow tangible trademarks add stability and strength to our beliefs. Let me tell you about one special symbol we are incorporating into the lives of our children.

When each of our sons turns sixteen, we give him a very special gift. It is a fourteen-carat gold key that symbolizes his sexual purity. It is to be worn around his neck on a gold chain until it is presented to his wife on their wedding night. It is a symbol of the virginity he has maintained while he waited for her—a promise that his body is hers and hers alone.

The key also represents the fact that we, as parents, are fully aware of the temptations and pressures that a young man faces every day in our society. It visualizes the promise that we will continuously pray for that child. It is a tangible expression of our expectations—not just our hopes—and a constant reminder to our son that God's way is different than the world's. They know that God has promised many blessings to those who live according to His rules and restrictions.

Originally the key was meant to be a silent pact between family members and later to be shared with their wives. In order to save them from the possible embarrassment or harassment of other sixteen-year-old males, we told our sons that if someone asked what it stood for, they could simply reply, "Oh, it's just something my parents gave me for my birthday."

However, things didn't go according to our script. When Zach, our oldest and therefore the first son to receive his key, was questioned on the day he received it, he blurted out his own reply: "It's a symbol of my virginity."

Because of his bluntness, no one dared question him any further at the time. "Cool," was about the only response he received. But from that day on, everyone knew exactly why he and his brothers wore keys around their necks. I have to be honest and tell you that some ridicule has accompanied that revelation. However, for the most part it has prompted great respect. The key has also provided several opportunities for our sons to share their faith and their views on sex and abstinence.

One funny incident associated with "the key" occurred during Zach's freshman orientation at college. He and several of his baseball teammates were attending a party when a girl spotted the key. She wondered out loud if the key symbolized a relationship he was "locked into" back home. Once again, Zach was brief, blunt, and honest. "No, it's a gift from my parents. It symbolizes my virginity, and I'm going to give it to my wife on my wedding night."

The girl's jaw dropped open, and she melted in front of him. "That's the sweetest thing I have ever heard in my life!" she exclaimed, then ran to get her friends so they could see Zach's key. Soon a dozen or more girls were surrounding Zach and checking out his key. As they left the party, one of his teammates grabbed him and said, "Diaz, that's the best line I've ever heard! Can I borrow your key?"

Raising children is the most challenging and rewarding task we as women can ever undertake. None of us can do it on our own. Not one of us has to. God offers us more power, promises, and joy for the job than we can ever imagine. But we can only appropriate them through prayer, and we can only learn of them by spending time in His Word. Each of us needs to grow in our own relationship with Him, and each of us needs to train our children to know Him to love, obey, and enjoy Him. We need to let our children grow up with God by their side.

Spirituality must be verbalized, symbolically reinforced, and lived out before our children, or it will never stand up to their scrutiny. It will fold when faced with their unanswered questions. It will crumble when hit by the challenges of our educational system. It will disintegrate under the pressures and pursuits of a teenager's life. We must no longer hope that God will somehow *fit* into our children's lives. We must allow Him to *fill* them!

❀ What mothering needs should I turn into prayer requests today?

❀ What are two things I can do today to help train my children to personally know God and experience His love?

✿ What are some things in my life that I need to change in order to make my "walk" live up to my "talk?"

A Mother's Prayer

Lord, I need Your help. I realize that I cannot handle the overwhelming responsibility of being a mom on my own. Yet, You have made the same power that created the entire universe available to me and my family. What an awesome thought! Please open the storehouses of Heaven and pour out Your love and joy and peace on us today. Guide me as I teach my children Your Word. Show me creative ways to concretely convey Your truths, and help my "walk" consistently back up my "talk." Give me a mighty heart, dear God, one that is empowered by You.

Endnotes

[1](p. 37) *Forever, Erma,* by Erma Bombeck (Kansas City: Andrews and McMeel,1996), p. 45.

[2](p. 62) *How to Really Love Your Child,* by Dr. Ross Campbell, M.D. (Wheaton: Victor Books, 1977) p. 33.

[3](p. 75) *Pilgrim Fathers . . . and Kids: The REAL Reason They Came to America,* by Charles Colson (BreakPoint Commentary #91124, 11/24/99).

[4](p. 136) *The Mudpies Book of Boredom Busters,* by Nancy Blakey (Tricycle Press, 1999).

[5](p. 137) *The Dubuque Telegraph Herald,* 'Dedicated potters present a "wheel" dose of Creativity,' by Shannon Hensen (April 11, 1999).

[6](p. 162) *Newsweek,* quoted in Case Studies by Dan Case May 29, 1998, (June 1. 1998) p. 20.

[7](pp. 166-167) *America, It's All in the Family,* by Joseph A. Califano Jr. (NY: Vol. 182; issue 2; Jan.15-22, 2000).

[8](pp. 178-179) *Laughter May Actually Be the Best Medicine* (*HealthCentral.com.,* March 31, 2000).

About the Author

Gwendolyn Mitchell Diaz's life
experiences emerge from a variety of
venues and vocations, all of which have
added tremendous insight and
background to her role as a mom. She
spent the first nine years of her life as a
"missionary kid," growing up in a mud
brick house with no electricity or
running water and attending boarding school in Nigeria,
West Africa. Her years adapting to life in the United States
included sports and scholarly pursuits.

A graduate of the University of Pennsylvania, Gwen
spent many years working in the medical profession while she
honed her writing skills and began her career as a mom. For
five years, she wrote a weekly newspaper column focusing on
the family issues and incidents that took place as she and her
husband, Ed, raised their four active sons.

Gwen's first book, *The Adventures of Mighty Mom*, was
published by RiverOak Publishing in March 2000. Her
writing and speaking engagements offer hope, help, and
humor as she encourages young women to enjoy the awesome
privileges and responsibilities of being a mom. She is
convinced that, with His help, God intended motherhood to
be a blast.

Additional copies of this book and other titles by RiverOak
Publishing are available from your local bookstore.

If you have enjoyed this book, or if it has impacted your
life, we would like to hear from you.

Please contact us at:

RiverOak Publishing
Department E
P.O. Box 700143
Tulsa, Oklahoma 74170-0143

Or by e-mail at info@riveroakpublishing.com

Visit our website at: www.riveroakpublishing.com